SIZE-POSITIVE STYLE!

CLOTHING FOR THE PLUS AND SUPERSIZE* WOMAN

*FAT
PHAT
ABUNDANT
HEALTHY
BIG
THICK
REAL
3D
BBW
GODDESS
LARGE
ZOFTIG
CURVY
FULL-FIGURED
FULL BODIED
REUBENESQUE
VOLUPTUOUS
CURVACEOUS
BODACIOUS

LINDA S. KANZINGER

THE ALCOTT PRESS
PORTLAND, OR

Published by The Alcott Press
6325 NE 7th Ave.
Portland, OR 97211-3601
503-287-3140
Email: alcottpres@aol.com
Website: http://www.Alcottpress.com

ISBN: 0-9616180-3-5

Printed in the United States of America
First Printing Summer 2001
10 9 8 7 6 5 4 3 2 1

Research, writing, typesetting and book production, book design, cover design and production, publishing, advertising and marketing by the author.

Permission is gratefully acknowledged for reprinting of the following quotes:
p. 45: From *Breaking All The Rules* by Nancy Roberts, copyright(c) 1985, 1986 , by Nancy Roberts. Used by permission of Viking Penguin, a division of Penguin Putnam, Inc.
p. 49: From *Breaking All The Rules* by Nancy Roberts, copyright(c) 1985, 1986 , by Nancy Roberts. Used by permission of Viking Penguin, a division of Penguin Putnam, Inc.
p. 56: From *Breaking All The Rules* by Nancy Roberts, copyright(c) 1985, 1986 , by Nancy Roberts. Used by permission of Viking Penguin, a division of Penguin Putnam, Inc.
p. 75: From *Style is Not a Size* by Hara Marano, Bantam Books, copyright 1991.
p. 77: From *Breaking All The Rules* by Nancy Roberts, copyright(c) 1985, 1986 , by Nancy Roberts. Used by permission of Viking Penguin, a division of Penguin Putnam, Inc.
p. 112: From *Art and Fashion in Clothing Selection* by Harriet McJimsey, Iowa State University Press, copyright 1973.
p. 112: From *Inside Fashion Design* by Sharon Lee Tate, Harper and Row copyright 1984. Reprinted by permission of Addison Wesley Educational Publishers, Inc.
p. 129: from *Color Me Beautiful* by Carole Jackson, Ballantine Books, a Division of Random House, Inc. copyright 1980.

Front cover: (upper left) Emanon wearing a navy blue suit with white collars and cuffs. Photo credit:Vic Toliva. (upper right) Ashley Taylor Clayton in a one piece denim dress with platform shoes. Photo credit: Satu. (lower left) Cleacia Foster in a black slipdress with gold sparkles. Photo credit: Skip Orlando. (lower right) Andrea Hall wears a 2 piece African print cloth outfit. Photo credit: Linda Kanzinger. (Back cover) Linda Kanzinger in purple and blue fold and dye African 2 piece outfit. Photo credit: Juanita Donaldson.

DEDICATION

DEDICATED TO ALL FAT WOMEN WHO ARE PROUD OF THEMSELVES THE WAY THEY ARE, AND TO ALL THE WOMEN IN THE SIZE-ACCEPTANCE MOVEMENT.

DEDICATED TO ALL FAT WOMEN WHO WISH THEY WERE OTHERWISE, IN THE HOPES THAT THEY WILL CHANGE THEIR MINDS— AFTER READING THIS BOOK!

TO MY FRIENDS WHO UNDERSTAND

AND

TO TIGER, TWINKLE, PACO, SABRINA, LILLY AND MOLLY, RABBI/D AND BONIDEA, AND THE "KIDS" : PETEY, BLOSSOM, LEPETITBELLE, AND FLOPPY DISK, AND L'IL PIGLET,

FOR KEEPING THIS

AUTHOR COMPANY WHILE ENJOYING THE SILENCE...

ACKNOWLEDGEMENTS

To all those who came before me, from whom I learned: Nancy Roberts, author of *Breaking all the Rules,* which started me on the road to discovering clothing for large women;publisher and founder Alice Ansfield of *Radiance: The Magazine for Large Women,* which I read while living in the backwaters of Spokane, WA, a magazine which decided to show reality when they not only wrote outstanding articles about and in celebration of large women, but also used plus-size models who went beyond the "acceptable" size 14-16; *NAAFA, The National Association to Advance Fat Acceptance,* Inc. for their continued fight against size discrimination and their awareness of issues for women of size, Carol Shaw, founding editor of *BBW magazine,* and Lisa Krebs, publisher, and Sally E Smith, Editor-in-Chief of the current *BBW Magazine*; Conrad and Ruby Blickenstorfer, Editor-In-Chief and VP Operations, concurrently, as well as Sandie Sabo, Social and Fashion Editor, all of *Dimensions Magazine,* who opened my eyes photographically to the supersize woman; Sonia Alleyne, editor-in-chief of *Belle Magazine,* who also has the courage to use the larger plus-size and the supersize model on their covers, when she can find them!

Special honors go to the wonderful Bill Fabrey, founder of NAAFA , networker extraordinare, currently my best email pal during this project, who always had names and numbers, suggestions and solicitations; also owner with Nancy Summer of a wonderful size-positive company, *Amplestuff* (www.amplestuff.com). I also want to thank local Portland pals Myra Turley, past president of the local *Portland NAAFA* chapter and friend, fashion maven extraordinare, who kept me current on all the new books, magazines, pattern companies, Internet sites, and small clothing manufacturers, and Mara Nesbitt-Aldrich, a great size-acceptance networker who educated me on the Internet, mailing lists, and in general held my hand in my first attempts at getting on-line. Thanks also to cyberspace genius Judy Sullivan, who puts out such an excellent website (www.sizewise.com) with so much networking and linking.

Thanks to all my models who participated in the book. Too numerous to name here, please check out the Index of Models in the Back Matter. Thanks also to my neighbor and friend Juanita Donaldson of Portland, Oregon, for her gracious hospitality in using her elegant home and yard for our photo shoots, as well as taking my final "author shot".

To Ted Cotrotsos and Despina Cotrotsos, Rosemarie McDowell, Emmy Chambers, and Pamela Allyn, thanks for translation services for some of the permission letters. Although I know some French, learning the Greek alphabet was too much of a challenge. Thanks, Despina! Thanks as well to both Ted Cotrotsos of Ted Cotrotsos Designs and Myra Turley for their help in critiquing the first phases of the book design.

Model captions:Forward: p. vi Kim Caldwell **Chapter I:** p 13 Sharon Klose (lower right) Cathy Bryant (lower left); p 14 Ashley Taylor Clayton, (lower left), Jennie Middleton (upper right), Cathy Bryant,(lower right); p 15 Gabrielle Sparapani (upper left) Andrea E. Cipala (upper right) Kim Caldwell and Nellie Steerns (bottom); p 16 Teresa Marie Metcalfe-Johnson (upper left) Cheryl Anderson, Bruce Bonnell (lower right); p.18 Cathy Bryant. **Photo credits Chapt I:** Sharon Klose: Perri Neri; Cathy Bryant: Linda Kanzinger, Ashley Taylor Clayton: Satu; Jennie Middleton:Heather Middleton of Shadowtint Photography, Teresa-Marie Metcalfe-Johnson: Satu; Cheryl Anderson, Bruce Bonnell: Linda Kanzinger.

PREFACE, OR WHY I DECIDED TO WRITE THIS BOOK

I decided to write this book for a number of reasons. One, as I grew older and a little heavier, I found I couldn't find sewing patterns that fit me without a lot of adjusting (and you know how time-consuming that is!). As I outgrew the size 14-16 pattern, and went into the size 18-20 range, there was also a psychological barrier, the shame of having to buy a size 18 pattern.

Size 18 conjured up in my mind pictures of drab, matronly looking women who looked depressed, wore "sensible shoes", had dull hairstyles, and looked beaten down by life in their brown and black shapeless clothing. I resisted, without even knowing why, and so for two summers I went without wearing shorts. I got by by wearing wide cotton casual skirts that still let my skin breathe, but it was an accommodation. When I played sports, I would wear long cotton pants. I found I missed bare legs, and the mobility that shorts give. Running, playing tennis, hiking, and bicycling in long pants simply was not as comfortable as in shorts.

I also found as I left my 20's and entered my 30's that I really didn't like wearing real tightfitting clothes anymore. I had been "squeezing" into the Mediums and Larges of manufactured clothing because that was all that was available. I wanted clothes that were comfortable, that fit well, that enhanced my figure, and that were appropriate to whatever situation I might be in. Even with the ability to sew my own clothes, I was finding that I just did not have the time nor interest to sew, adapt patterns, and make patterns,—all of which I had done at one time or another. I wanted clothes that fit, that were pretty, enhanced my appearance, and even with my ability to sew, it wasn't working. I wanted to be able to go to the store and buy clothes, just like everybody else!

As this consciousness began to break open in me, I realized that there were a lot of women in a much worse position than I was, in that they were larger than me (more than 5'4", 203 lbs), and without sewing skills. **I began to think: "what on earth were they doing for a wardrobe?" I was in denial in that I never even thought: "why can't I go shopping for clothes just like my average-size friends do?"**

EVEN WITH THE ABILITY TO SEW MY OWN CLOTHES, I WAS FINDING THAT I JUST DID NOT HAVE THE TIME NOR INTEREST TO SEW, ADAPT PATTERNS, AND MAKE PATTERNS,ALL OF WHICH I HAD DONE AT ONE TIME OR ANOTHER. I WANTED CLOTHES THAT FIT, THAT WERE PRETTY, ENHANCED MY APPEARANCE, AND EVEN WITH MY ABILITY TO SEW, IT WASN'T WORKING. I WANTED TO BE ABLE TO GO TO THE STORE AND BUY CLOTHES, JUST LIKE EVERYBODY ELSE!

At the same time that this was happening to me on an individual level, I also noticed what was called—in the late 1980's, the Big is Beautiful movement, and what is now known as the size-acceptance, or fat-acceptance movement. I began to read magazines like *BBW* and *Radiance*, go to conventions put on by NAAFA (The National Association to Advance Fat Acceptance). I was excited to find a growing movement to end discrimination for fat women and men. All this put me more and more in touch with my own feelings about being big. It inspired me to seek out the available literature on plus and supersize women. I read what was available, and the ideas began to flow. I studied phat women's issues from the late eighties into the early nineties, and noticed a continual evolvement of fashionable clothing available to us.

I originally decided to focus on handcrafted clothing for full-bodied women for this book. However, writing has its own direction, and I found that, as I researched, I didn't find enough information to pursue this thoroughly. As I continued my research, it shifted direction towards clothing in general. What remains here is a book which first presents size-positive images of fat women, then shows a variety of our body shapes, then explains the basics of fashion principles while illustrating the text with large, lovely bodacious women wearing successful designs.The book then ends with a presentation of various styles that women can choose to express a certain feeling or for a specific occasion. Several appendices highlight the models and artists, along with a bibliography and other size-positive resources.

The actual final work of this book took a full two years—with long work hours, approximating 55 hour weeks at times. I encountered numerous "challenges" which could be interpreted as size discrimination. Hard to prove in some cases, obvious in others, such as apparent censorship from a book printer with whom I had previously had a pleasant working relationship, who could accept a partially clothed figure of a woman by Renoir but not a similar image from a current "modern"artist.

For every historical art image, countless hours were spent first finding images of fat women in art books and elsewhere, then writing to various places for permission to reproduce. In the past museums would forward the original address of the person/institution that owned the artwork, and they usually would graciously send back a letter saying "yes", simply asking for a credit line.

This time, however, it was like pulling teeth to get permission for reproduction of classic art images of zoftig women. Policies have changed. I was shocked at how many institutions such as major museums simply never answered correspondence with repeated attempts ignored.There was no logic to this: the Louvre answered quickly and graciously, while a similar art institute in the US never responded. Or, they sent a letter that basically dead-ended the search, stating that they no longer owned the piece of art. They have to have a record, I would think, but none was forthcoming. Was this due to the title, and content, of the book? I will never know.

Permission for quotes sometimes was similarly discouraging. In spite of copyright law of " fair use", which allows up to 300 words, one publisher wanted $50.00 for me to quote 15 words in a sidebar!

On the other hand, there was the wonderful connection through the Internet of hundreds of women who wanted to participate in the book. I corresponded with many women, and chose from numerous images the best and the most voluptuous!!! In no other way could I have had the variety of models without this medium.

I also attempted to make this book multi-ethnic. Although I researched, signed up on message boards, and attempted to get the word out to the Black, Latina, Indian, and Asian communities, I did not reach my vision of a multi-ethnic group of models. I'll try again in the next book.

Size-Positive Style! Clothing for the Plus and Supersize Woman* extols all large women and calls us to see ourselves as beautiful: womanly, warm, sensual. We need no longer buy into the popular ideology that "thin is in". In fact, thin can be seen as squawky, gangly, awkward, while fat is stately, honorable, smooth. Sometimes it's necessary to push back. We have been pushed on and put down far too long.

WOMEN.

DON T EAT.

DON T FEED YOURSELF.

DON T NOURISH YOURSELF.

RESTRAIN YOUR APPETITES.

BE

THE RIGHT SIZE.

TABLE OF CONTENTS

INTRODUCTION

"GAUNT, FRAIL-LOOKING MODELS WITH STICK ARMS AND FENCEPOST LEGS, NO SIGN OF WOMANLINESS ANYWHERE..."

"WOMANLY BREASTS AND HIPS OBLITERATED IN FAVOR OF A SKELETAL LOOK..."

Would this be a role model in a country full of starvation? Hardly so. It is the irony that, in a country with accessible food —to most all— skeletal images abound as " the ideal" image of woman.

This book takes a stand against this image that is promulgated, obliterating the images of real women who live, walk, work, eat, love, have full lives. Those women, now stated at 55% overweight, and 20% obese, with another 10% "morbidly" obese— are obliterated in favor of this skeletal image of womanness: bone, bone and more bone on which are draped clothes. No wonder they are called clothes-hanger women.

The women in this book, as a quick glance will tell, are not skeletal. They are full bodied women. They have curves— they have breasts and hips, and they are not afraid of showing them. Sometimes they flaunt these womanly curves. This is in full opposition of the cultural norm that has, for some time, convinced women and the society at large that to be a woman is to be thin. To be healthy is to be thin. To be acceptable is to be thin.

Not so, and these size-positive women claim the opposite: to live full lives in their full bodies, to have partners and sexuality and pretty clothes and lives and jobs and activities. We are not the "morbidly obese" though the insurance companies would have us so, and deny many of us insurance based upon one little number: the BMI (determined only by height and weight, nothing else).

This book claims: not so! We are riding bikes, skiing, lifting weights, dancing, hiking. We are joyous and active in our full bodies. We are women of high self-esteem. We are size-positive women!

Turn these pages, and enjoy the merging of the size-positive woman and pretty clothes. Enjoy these images from art herstory as well as the current artists who paint, again in some defiance, from the cultural norms, the full-bodied figure. The Reubenesque, bodacious, curvaceous figure. The Goddess. All of these size-positive words replace less celebratory ones: chunky, chubby, heavyset, plump.

But there is one word we have reclaimed, and that is the word " fat". Fat is not a four-letter word. It is not an insult, unless you would have it so. Fat describes softness. It is cushiony; it describes bounce, abundance, substance.

After ten years of research, watching an ever-growing industry and trying to wrap my arms around it and "get a handle" on it, after talking with many many people, being involved with NAAFA: The National Association to Advance Fat Acceptance, reading magazines like Belle, BBW, Radiance, and Dimensions, reading powerful books on size discrimination such as *The Invisible Woman* by W. Charisse Goodman, and especially getting on-line and checking out the hundreds of fat-acceptance sites on-line, especially enjoying the sites of Love Your Peaches, and its photogenic owner/designer Janelle Bonlie,also Judy Sullivan's "site magnifique"! www.sizewise.com, and Reuben's Way(www.theviproom.com/rubensnest); joining mailing lists such as the fat-acceptance mailing list (majordomo@world.std.com subscribe fat-acceptance) with friendly help from its administrator, Charlie Van Dyke, exploring the many sites on the BBW Webring and the BBW/FA Ring and learning from other fat people about the issues they deal with, including clothing, after learning myself how to dress well and celebrate my older bigger body as opposed to my younger less big body, still always mine, and in my eyes, always pretty (regardless that most people never agreed with me, I always thought it true),

I now present to you,

my book,

nurtured in years of watching fat women, learning how they dressed, seeing the size-positive ones apart from the ones who agreed with the culture's definition of them as invisible, asexual, and not worth human dignity,

I present to you this book,

Twelve years in the making, grown into chapters, but then more information, new growth in fat-acceptance, as activists fought in the courts for human rights, for the right to work in their chosen career even if they gained weight, not to be fired, as Sharon Klose did in the nursing field, taking it all the way up to the Supreme Court, many conversations with Bill Fabrey who connected me with many wonderful people, some of whom are pictured in this book, more information until finally, finally, I had what I stood strong on: visual images of phat women dressed attractively and in their style and personality all their own, women who were of high self-esteem, the size-positive woman. I had held the line, asking for models who were large, at least wearing a size 20W. Soliciting for photos a number of years earlier brought many pictures, but most were wearing size 12. Maybe size 14. This was not my definition of "plus-size". Maybe for others— maybe for the whole world. But not my definition. I look at Mode magazine and I see average-sized women. I am told they are "plus-size" Then where are the average-sized women if average-looking women are defined as "more-than" (plus) size? Is the average-size woman now a slender woman? It would seem so, if we look around at the world we inhabit, whether it is in the health field or the fashion world. But this is not my belief.

So I stood strong. I also had another requirement for my book— that the women were beautiful in the physical sense. I was told that the fat-acceptance movement wouldn't like this, because I was not "politically correct" as all BBW's are beautiful. This is important for self-esteem, but for me, there is beauty of spirit and beauty of the flesh. To say that all women are beautiful means the same to me as to say all women are ugly. It is a generalization and none holds true. So for this book, my book, I wanted fat women who were beautiful. And I held the line, until I got what I wanted: big beautiful women with high self-esteem: the size-positive woman.

So I introduce to you,

my book:

Size-Positive Style! Clothing for the Plus and Supersize Woman.*

May it change your world, as it has mine.

1

SIZE POSITIVE STYLE! WHO IS THE SIZE-POSITIVE WOMAN?

She is a woman who is proud of her size. She likes to wear clothes that show the shape of her body. She feels good about her body. Maybe not all at once, maybe not in every situation, every time, but overall she has come to accept her body as it is—without reservation, and often with celebration.

The way she dresses, the way she carries herself, reveals a size-positive attitude.

WHETHER YOU ARE WORKING IN A HOME OFFICE ON A COMPUTER...

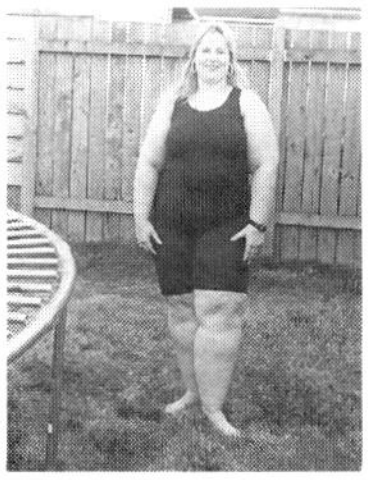

WHETHER YOU ARE GRADUATING FROM COLLEGE...

OR A WINNER IN A BEAUTY QUEEN PAGEANT...

OR ON A VACATION IN HAWAII READY TO BOARD A CRUISE SHIP...

WHETHER PUMPING GAS IN A PRETTY DRESS AND HAT....

OR JUST HAVING A GOOD BELLY LAUGH AT A BIRTHDAY PARTY...

"I HAVE A SIMPLE QUESTION TO ASK YOU.

IS YOUR BIG BODY BAD?

WHEN YOU SAY YOU ARE PEAR SHAPED AND SO OF COURSE YOU ARE GOING TO WEAR DARK COLORS—THE BLACKS— ON THE BOTTOM, AND

WEAR THE BRIGHT COLORS ABOVE YOUR WAIST...

WHAT I HEAR YOU SAYING IS THAT

BIG IS BAD!!

IS YOUR BIG BODY BAD?

IF YOU DON'T WEAR A-LINES, OR BIG PRINTS, OR GATHERED SKIRTS BECAUSE THEY MAKE YOU LOOK BIGGER...

ARE YOU SAYING:

MY BIG BODY IS BAD!!!!

I WANT TO SEE PEAR SHAPED WOMEN WEARING LEMON COLORED SLACKS THAT

SHOW THEIR CURVES."

2

SIZE-POSITIVE IMAGES OF WOMEN

CONTRARY TO TODAY'S MADNESS, there has always been a celebration of the fuller figure. In countries where food is not readily available, the fuller figure is seen as "high status", whereas in this country the plus and supersize woman endures low status. Painters have always painted the lush female form. Sometimes they used pregnant women in order to have models with rounded tummies. Others were chosen because of their rounded stomachs and full breasts, ample thighs, big hips.

They were Woman epitomized.

(below) "Ode aux fleurs" (Ode to Flowers) -Pierre-Auguste Renoir. 17.9"x 14 ". Paris, Musee d'Orsay in deposit in municipal Musee of Limoges, 1986. (right) Chalk and pencil drawing done of Cleacia Foster in the image of an angel by Paul Delacroix. 11" x 14". © 1999 by Paul Delacroix.

(above left) "Apples from Venus"- by Dimitri Kare. 13" x 19", gouache on French rag watercolor paper. Though much of Dimitri's work is influenced by classical Greek and Renaissance art, he is ultimately interested in timeless aspects of life and beauty. © Dimitri Kare.(above right) "Pear Shaped Woman"- T'Rina Headlee. 8" by 11". Pencil drawing. An meditative or yoga-like pose of a figure with Indian or Native American features. © 1999 T'Rina Headlee. (below) "Watercolor" by T'Rina Headlee. 8" x 11". Watercolor on paper in blues, purples, and lavender. This figure in repose upon the ground, clearly shows the full smooth curves of the fat female body. © 1999 T'Rina Headlee.

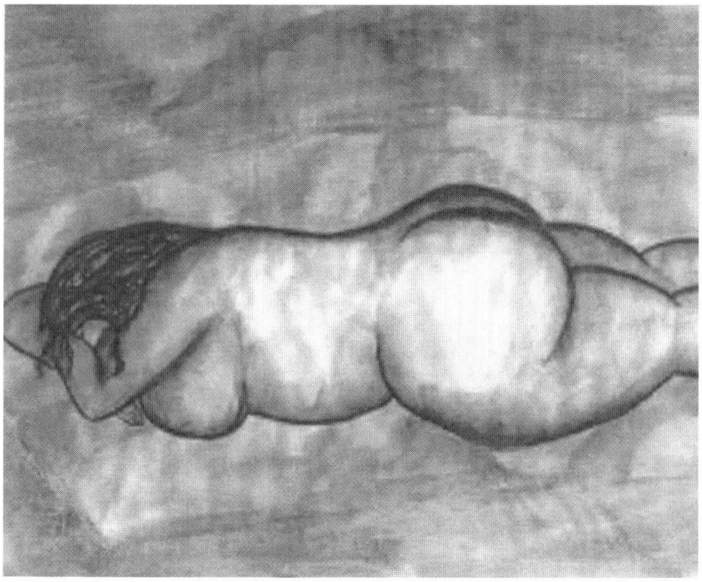

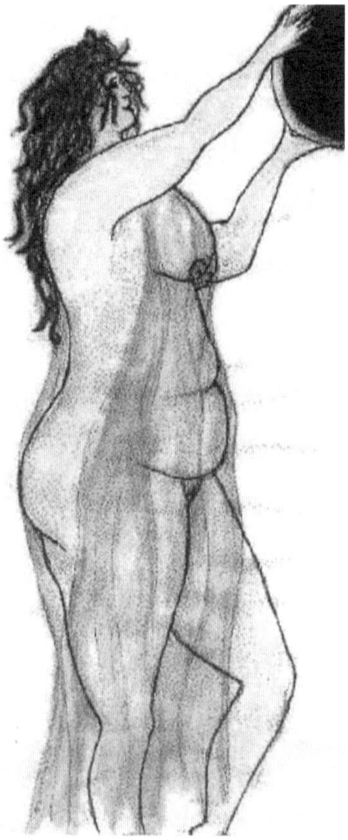

(Above left) "Eclipse"- T'Rina Headlee. 8" by 11 ". Line drawing with watercolor wash. © 1999 T'Rina Headlee.

(Above) "Fairy"- Dimitri Kare. Stamp image from pen and ink/computer drawing. © Dimitri Kare.

(above right) " Staffeli Dame"("Easel Lady")- Lis Gede. 21cm by 29 cm. Ink and touche on paper.©1999 by Lis Gede. (lower right) "With Eyes Towards Mocca"- Lis Gede. 69 cm by 89 cm. Oil on canvas. ©1993 by Lis Gede.

(above) "Vandkande Dame" (Waterpitcher Woman)-Lis Gede. 21 cm by 29 cm. Ink and touche on paper. This lyrical rendition of a lovely curvaceous big woman is representative of the body shape of the Supersize Scallop. The sexy earthiness of the figure is reflected in the thematic material of earth and flowers, shown in the draped flowered gown , her toes dug into the earth, and the general setting for the figure. © 1999 by Lis Gede.

(above)"Venus on Green"- by Dimitri Kare. 17" x 22". Gouache on watercolor paper. © Dimitri Kare. (lower right) "Spring and Autumn"- Dimitri Kare. 9" x 11", gouache on watercolor paper, © Dimitri Kare. (below) "Angel with Flowers"- by Dimitri Kare. Stamp image from pen and ink/computer drawing.© Dimitri Kare.

(above) "Bicycle Girl"- Paul Delacroix. ©1999 by Paul Delacroix.

(above) "Gold line Study # 1" - T'Rina Headlee. 8" x 11".Gold Prismacolor pencil line drawing on black paper. ©1999 T'Rina Headlee. (below) " Silver line Study # 1- T'Rina Headlee. 8" x 11". Silver Prismacolor pencil line drawing on black paper. ©1999 T'Rina Headlee.

(below) "Catnap"- Dimitri Kare. Stamp image from pen and ink/computer drawing. © Dimitri Kare.

A number of new artists have been highlighted in this chapter. It is wonderful to me to see current artists painting the fat form. Their interpretations and representations of the plus and supersize woman is exciting, and long overdue! With a wide variation in style, all the artists show a size-positive attitude towards the abundant form.

Images of the fat women in art herstory can only increase in the future!

3

PRINCIPLES AND PRECEPTS:

THE UNDERPINNING OF MY PHILOSOPHY ON FAT WOMEN AND CLOTHING

Over time, I developed certain principles that guided me in understanding what I feel works for plus and supersize women as far as clothing goes. I decided to call these my precepts, because they are the underpinnings of my entire philosophy about clothes and fat women. I think they are important, and this is why I am giving them a separate chapter.

#1
EVERY BODY IS OK

WHAT DOES THIS MEAN? IT MEANS THAT, FOR ME, EVERYBODY'S BODY IS OK.

WHATEVER YOUR IN-SHAPE, YOUR OUT-OF-SHAPE, YOUR SIZE, YOUR BIGNESS, THE NUMBER ON THE SCALE, YOUR BODY IS OK.

THAT HAS TO BE THE STARTING POINT,

BUT IT DOESN'T HAVE TO BE THE ENDING POINT. BUT WHEREVER YOU MOVE ALONG THE CONTINUUM, YOUR BODY IS OK.

WHATEVER YOUR BODY IS.

#2

DESIGN CLOTHES TO FIT THE BODY, DON'T DESIGN THE BODY TO FIT THE CLOTHES.

I''LL SAY IT OVER AND OVER AGAIN. THINK OF DESIGNING CLOTHES TO FIT THE BODIES THAT **WE ALREADY HAVE,** RATHER THAN TRYING TO GET US TO DESIGN OUR BODIES TO FIT THE CLOTHES **THAT ALREADY ARE.** DESIGN CLOTHES THAT FIT US **NOW.** IT'S CHALLENGING, CREATIVE, AND FUN.

#3

WE HAVE TO CHANGE THE ESSENTIAL CONCEPT OF CLOTHES!

What this means is that what we see in the sewing catalogues, in stores, and in catalogues and fashion magazines are clothes primarily designed for bodies that are not shaped like ours. Since **our** clothes are designed for **our** bodies, then our clothes are somewhat different from what we've all come to think of as the idea of **what clothes are.**

We can throw away those ideas that don't fit! We can and will embrace the styles of **clothes** that are **designed** for **our bodies.** For us, those are what clothes are. That other stuff—now irrelevant!

#4

DRESS FOR THE OCCASION.

THIS IS MORE COMPLEX THAN IT LOOKS. IT MEANS LEARNING HOW TO PUT TOGETHER OUTFITS SO THAT YOU WILL FEEL, AND BE, APPROPRIATELY DRESSED FOR THE SITUATION IN WHICH YOU FIND YOURSELF.

MOST RADICAL IS A SLEEVELESS TOP ON A HOT SUMMER DAY, COMBINED WITH SHORTS AND SANDALS OR TENNIS SHOES, AND POSSIBLY A STRAW HAT TO WARD OFF THE SUN. A SLEEVELESS SUNDRESS, OR A SEE-THROUGH GAUZY LAYERED OUTFIT PROVIDES MORE "SECURITY," WHILE STILL BEING APPROPRIATELY DRESSED FOR THE OCCASION.

#5

WE CAN CHOOSE TO HIGHLIGHT AND SHOW EMPHASIS, OR DE-EMPHASIZE, ANY PART OF OUR BODY.

This means the concept of "proportion" is outdated—always having to "balance" the figure to approach the "ideal". Since there is an implied value of appropriate body shapes/size imposed upon us, it is assumed in most fashion books that we would want to "hide" large hips, large stomachs, "too" large bosoms, thick waists.

I state that this is our choice. Some of us will want to proportion our figure to approach an ideal "balanced" figure, and often be aware of balancing so-called "figure faults"; others of us will revel in showing all parts of our bodies at various times, highlighting the thick ankles or the large stomach.

We all have body features that we like best about ourselves. We can look sexy and attractive with these features: a voluptuous bosom, a curvy silhouette, strong big arms.

It really is more of the whole than the parts. Some of us are going to look better following one set of ideas, and others are going to look better or express their personality being more "free" in their approach.

#6

MY PRINCIPLE OF REVEALING AND CONCEALING:

THE MORE YOU WANT TO REVEAL YOUR EXACT BODY SHAPE AND CURVE, THE MORE YOU WILL WANT TO WEAR FABRIC WHICH IS FLEXIBLE, KNIT, UNSTRUCTURED, STRETCHY, DRAPING.

AND THE INVERSE:

THE LESS YOU WANT TO REVEAL YOUR EXACT BODY SHAPE AND CURVE, THE MORE YOU WANT TO WEAR FABRIC WHICH IS WOVEN, STIFF, STRUCTURED, STURDY, AND SHAPED.

FAT IS NOT A FOUR LETTER WORD

FAT IS A DESCRIPTION OF PART OF OUR LARGE BODIES. WE CAN BE **BIG, LARGE, FAT, STOCKY, MUSCULAR, CURVY.** THERE IS **A BIAS AGAINST FAT IN AMERICA** THAT IS NOT SHARED AROUND THE WORLD. THERE IS **A MORAL JUDGMENT AGAINST FAT PEOPLE** AT THIS POINT IN TIME. OUR BODY SHAPES INCLUDE BONE, MUSCLE, FAT, AND SKIN. SOME OF US ARE MORE FAT THAN OTHERS. SOME OF US WHO ARE LARGE HAVE BIGGER BONE STRUCTURE AND LESS FAT, BUT WE ARE ALSO SEEN AS LARGE.**THERE ARE MANY COMBINATIONS.**

FAT IS NOT A FOUR-LETTER WORD. IT IS A DESCRIPTION OF PART OF OUR BODIES.

THE LIE

Dear Friends,

I must write and tell you something strange from the 20th century.

People are going around taking pictures of women who are average sized, and calling them "plus" sized.

Do you remember when you and I used to sew, and a size 12 was a "medium"? A size 16-18 was a "large" size?

But now women who are a medium size from a long time ago, such as in the middle of the last century, are considered "plus" size!

Just thought you would want to know the goings on from this planet.

Yours Truly,
Size-Positive Style

REVEALING THE ROUNDED BODY STEP BY STEP

SINCE OUR SOCIETY LAUGHS AT OUR ROUNDED BODIES, IT TAKES SOME TIME TO "COME OUT".

WEARING CLOTHES THAT ARE NOT REVEALING IN THE MORE CRITICIZED PARTS OF OUR BODIES IS CERTAINLY UNDERSTANDABLE. SOMETIMES, IN ORDER TO AVOID THE STRESS, IT IS SIMPLY EASIER TO NOT CONFRONT THE PREJUDICE.

OTHER TIMES, IT IS LIBERATING TO COME OUT, TO WEAR REVEALING CLOTHES, ESPECIALLY REVEALING THINGS LIKE BIG ROUND STOMACHS, OR ROLLS OF FAT ABOVE THE WAIST, OR "FLAPPER" UPPER ARMS.

I M NOT ADVOCATING THAT EVERYONE SHOULD SAY:THIS IS BEAUTIFUL.

I AM NOT PART OF A MOVEMENT WHICH STATES THAT THE FATTER A BODY IS, THE MORE BEAUTIFUL THE BODY.

WHAT I AM SAYING IS THAT EACH OF US, INDIVIDUALLY, HAS OUR TOLERANCE LEVEL OF WHAT WE WANT TO REVEAL.

BY REVEALING MORE OF OUR ROUNDED BODIES, A STEP AT A TIME, WE CAN EACH FIND OUR OWN COMFORT LEVEL AND FIND INDIVIDUAL STYLE FOR OURSELVES.

NOW FOR ME, THAT'S BEAUTIFUL!

THE POLITICS OF SIZING

"Size 26 is now a supersize.
As I say,
big
is getting smaller
all the time."

Linda Kanzinger-*Size-Positive Style*

I REFUSE TO BELIEVE

THAT 2% IS

THE REALITY

Think about what it would be like if we lived in a country where we really looked at **real people,** and derived standards from them, instead of having images of women dominate us from pages of magazines. These silkscreened images are manipulated to show the 2%, ie, a minority of women, dominating the **perception** of what is the norm for the majority of women! Kind of odd, isn't it?

I REFUSE TO BELIEVE

THAT 2% IS

"THE NORM"

AND THAT

98%

IS

DEVIANT!

SELF-ESTEEM

The first principle or the first thing is to feel good about yourself. If you don't feel good about yourself, you aren't going to look good. And your clothes aren't going to look good.

If you are dressing to slenderize...

If you are dressing to camouflage...

If you are dressing in black...

If you are squeezing into too-tight clothes because you can't face going up another size...

you need to work on your self-esteem

HOW TO ACCOMPLISH THIS?

YOUR BODY IS OK.

EVERY BODY IS OK.

This is your mantra.

Repeat it every morning when you wake up.

Repeat it before you get dressed.

Repeat it throughout the day.

YOUR BODY IS OK
JUST THE WAY IT IS NOW.

As Myra Turley, Past President of Portland, Oregon's NAAFA Chapter states,

"You don't want to look thinner. You want to look good!!!"

(right) Myra Turley wearing a periwinkle rayon print pants with co-ordinated rayon shirt, size 4 from Making It Big. Photo credit: Linda Kanzinger.

PROPORTION

Let's blow this one out of the water right now!

Proportion is a fashion principle that has been distorted way out of line, especially when we start talking about plus and super sizes!

Proportion is supposed to make your 5'4" 250 lb body look thinner, right? Wearing black hose is supposed to "slim" your thick muscular calves?

I don't know about you, but I don't think we have any miracle surgeries here. My thick muscular calves are thick and wide regardless of whether or not I am wearing black hose, white hose, or no hose.

Proportion. "We" are "supposed" to want to have our bodies appear as close to the "ideal form" as possible. So if we have big busts, we are supposed to "balance" that bigness with big hips, and woe if we don't have big hips, we wear thickly gathered skirts.

On the other hand, if we have big hips and a small bust, we are "supposed" to wear shoulder pads to "balance out" and thereby "maintain proportion". Let's see, 2+2=4! That's it.

WHO ARE YOU KIDDING?

I WANT TO LOOK LIKE ME, NOT LIKE SOME GREEK STATUE—

SOME ANCIENT FIGURE BASED ON THE IDEAL PROPORTIONS OF A DEAD PERSON!

A LITTLE STORY

SHERRY AT PS TOLD ME SHE HEARD ON THE RADIO THAT SIZE 10 IS NOW DEEMED A "PLUS SIZE".

I TOLD LYNN AT THE LIBRARY.

"WHAT'S IT GOING TO BE IN FIVE YEARS?" SHE ASKED.

"I'M A SIZE **NEGATIVE 6?"**

Thanks to Lynn Hale of Portland, Oregon for this mind-scintillating comment!

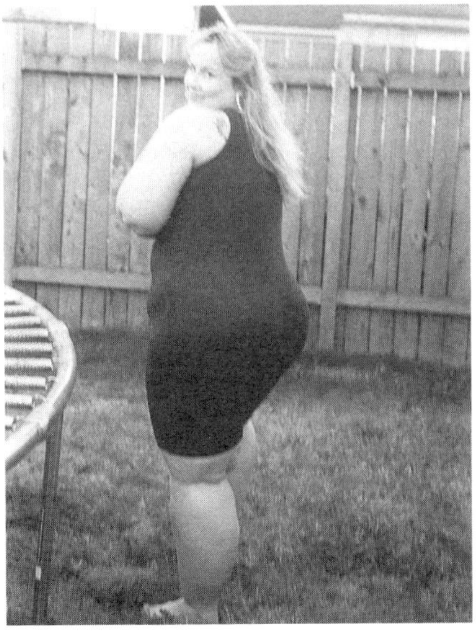

" I WEAR a size 22

I AM NOT a size 22

Since when did

my SIZE

become

my IDENTITY?"

Size-Positive Style- Linda S.

SIZE-POSITIVE RIGHTS!

EVERY TIME A WOMAN OF SIZE STEPS INTO PUBLIC VIEW WEARING BRIGHT COLORS, CLOTHING THAT SHOWS HER TRUE SHAPE, HORIZONTAL STRIPES AND BRIGHT PRINTS, AND HAS A POSITIVE ATTITUDE ABOUT HERSELF AND HER LOOKS, SHE IN ESSENCE IS A ROLE MODEL FOR WOMEN WHO HAVEN'T QUITE GOTTEN TO "SIZE-POSITIVE".

OF COURSE, AS A SIZE-POSITIVE WOMAN OF SUBSTANCE, SHE ALSO HAS THE RIGHT TO FEEL DOWN, TO NOT STEP OUT ALL BRIGHT AND PERKY EVERYDAY, TO NOT HAVE A POSITIVE ATTITUDE AND CONFIDENT STEP, THE SAME RIGHT THAT EVERY THIN AND AVERAGE SIZED WOMAN ASSUMES.

MUCH TO THE CHAGRIN AND DISAPPROVAL OF THE FASHION ESTABLISHMENT, SHE, LIKE HER THINNER SISTERS, ALSO HAS THE RIGHT TO NOT BE "IMPECCABLY GROOMED" EVERY TIME SHE GOES OUT THE DOOR.

SHE ALSO HAS THE RIGHT TO WEAR BLACK AS A FASHION STATEMENT JUST LIKE EVERY OTHER HUMAN BEING, AND NOT WITH THE DANGLING "SO SLENDERIZING" COMMENT MADE BY SOME SALES CLERKS.

IN SHORT, SHE HAS THE RIGHT

TO BE

A FULL HUMAN BEING

IN A FULL HUMAN BODY.

4

TRADITIONAL RULES OF DRESSING FOR PLUS AND SUPERSIZE WOMEN—

AND HOW AND WHY TO BREAK THEM

" THE RULES ARE FASHIONED IN SUCH A WAY TO PRESUPPOSE THAT EVERYONE WANTS THE IDEAL FIGURE, AND THE CLOSER ONE COMES TO THE IDEAL FIGURE, THE BETTER.

In books on fashion design, it is very common to see, along with a discussion of silhouette and clothing components, a discussion of the "rules of fashion" (to be subsequently described by me as The Rules)— the shoulds and should nots. Usually, this is divided into body parts: if your breasts are too big, do this, and don't do that. Or, if you have narrow shoulders, wear this and this, but don't wear that.

There are reasons for these rules: they conform to an underlying ideology that says that there is such a thing as an "ideal" figure; and by emphasizing or minimizing certain parts of ones' figure, a person can attempt to approximate the "ideal" figure.

The Rules have the presupposition that it is the ideal figure that everyone wants, and the closer one comes to the ideal figure, the better. Everything that is not the ideal figure is called a figure flaw.

From this comes the terminology of "too big" and "too small" (breasts, waists, hips, shoulders, thighs, etc). Some books specifically focus on how to dress to look two sizes smaller, or how to dress to hide figure flaws. *Sleek Chic* by Tracy Hensler, *Flatter Your Figure* by Jan Larkey, *Dressing Thin* by Dale Goday, and *The Complete Bonnie August Dress Thin System* by Bonnie August are several such books.

THEREFORE, EVERYTHING THAT IS NOT THE 'IDEAL FIGURE' IS CALLED A 'FIGURE FLAW' "

"Not all designs work on large bodies, but then not all designs work on average or small size bodies. This is why the concept of approaching the plus and supersize woman as a unique shape is so much more refreshing than trying to have her squeeze into a box of restrictive rules"

One of the most common chapters to find in books on fashion and design is one that talks about "The Rules". Some of these books include: *It's You, Looking Terrific*, and *Always in Style* by Emily Cho; *Dressing Rich*, and *Dress Like a Million* both by Leah Feldman, *Dress with Style* by Janet Wallace, *Conservative Chic* by Amelia Fatt, and *Style Strategy* by Jane Segerstrom, among others.

While these books in general have some reasonable advice for the average size women, they are very discouraging and insulting to the plus and supersize woman. Everything is termed as a "don't: don't wear this, don't wear that." Many times the rules overlap, and if we were to sincerely follow these rules, we would end up wearing nothing! (Now I don't think they would really like us to do that!)

These rules, while quite popular, are not written in stone. They can be challenged. Unfortunately, they have also crept into several of the plus-size fashion books. They are tenacious! Since they have been echoed in book after book, they tend to become "set", and then clothing designers and manufacturers oblige by following them as well.

"I propose that we throw out the rules, and begin again. This will lead us to a discussion of 'fashion principles' rather than rules."

If we think of the concept of "unique" rather than "ideal", we can begin instead with the natural body silhouette of each individual large woman, and work outward into which kinds of existing designs will look good on her. Many of the newer clothes in the plus-size women's clothing stores are your traditional designs: silk, rayon, and cotton blouses; straight skirts, A-line skirts, shirtwaist dresses.

It is now obvious to designers that many designs work well on large bodies, as well as an average or small sized bodies. Interestingly enough, before the movement towards clothing for phat women, designers and manufacturers simply insisted that small size patterns absolutely could not be graded up to large sizes.

"Yet now the plus size market contains many **traditional designs**—and the supersize market is growing! It appears that it was the **prejudice** of the **designers** towards **the plus-size body**, and not **the nuts and bolts** of **designing**, that caused them to state what they did regarding **sizing**."

Not all designs work on large bodies, but then not all designs work on average or small size bodies. This is why the concept of approaching the plus and supersize woman as a unique shape is so much more refreshing than trying to have her squeeze into a box of restrictive rules.

Just for a look backwards, let's look at what some fashion writers have stated about the fashion rules. Although the following is a compilation from a number of fashion books, these Rules were pretty much "in the air"; ie no one person came up with them. They seem to have been the "common wisdom regarding the plus and supersize woman" before the plus and supersize fashion movement took hold.

(above) Flirtatious Myra Turley poses in her 100% cotton denim front-button shirtwaist dress, brass buttons, size 4, with rayon animal print scarf. Photo credit: Linda Kanzinger.

"ALL THE WOMEN STRESSED WHAT A DIFFERENCE IT MADE TO THEM WHEN THEY WERE GIVEN THE CHANCE TO DRESS NORMALLY, TO WEAR SOMETHING THEY REALLY LIKED, SOMETHING WITH STYLE"

Nancy Roberts: *Breaking All The Rules*

(right) Rulerbreaker Cleacia Foster wows us in her shirtwaist cotton blend shirt size 26/28W, worn with stretch bluejeans, size 22/24W. You can't get sexier than this!!! ("No Tight Clothes" Rule is Broken!) Photo credit: Skip Orlando.

TRADITIONAL RULES FOR PLUS AND SUPERSIZE WOMEN

FOR LARGE-FRAMED, FULL-FIGURED WOMEN

No tent dresses
Nothing skintight
No large expanses of bold pattern
No front-pleated trousers
No dirndl skirts
No pleated skirts
No front-pleated skirts
No tight clothes
No large clothes
No heavy bulky wools
No jersey fabrics
No clingy fabrics
No bold patterns
No shiny fabrics
No plaids (makes big hips look wider)
No oversize shoulders
No sleeveless styles
No strapless styles

FOR WIDE, BROAD, AND SQUARE SHOULDERS

No dolman sleeves
No cap sleeves
No puff sleeves
No sleeveless looks
No shoulder pads
No horizontal lines at the waist
No horizontal patterns

"Rulebreaker" Cat Nordling in a gorgeous gingham shirtwaist —a blue and black plaid with black ribbon trim. The fabric of this dress is rayon and poly/blend crepe, from PS, Plus Sizes, Size 4X. ("No Horizontal Lines for Big Hips" Rule Broken !!!)Think what you would miss out on if you followed these silly rules! Cat enhances this outfit with a blue wool felt hat, one size, from PS, Plus Sizes. Photo credit: Staci Gilbert.

FOR HEAVY ARMS

No tight-fitting sleeves
No clinging fabrics
No sleeveless sleeves
No strapless sleeves
No snug knits
No sweater knits

FOR LARGE BUST

No horizontal stripes or lines
No wide belts
No tight-fitting waists or horizontal lines at the waist
No fitted jackets
No tight or clinging tops
No cowlneck sweaters
No shiny or heavy fabrics
No light colored tops with a dark skirt or pants
No hanging pendants on your bust
No yokes, piping, pockets, or other detail around the yoke

FOR A LARGE OR THICK WAIST

No colors which change at the waist
No to most belts without something to hide the waist—ie an overjacket or vest.
No A-line skirts
No princess lines

SHORT WAIST

No wide belts
No two colors that meet at the waist (ie separates in differing colors), with an emphasis at the waist

(above) "Rulebreaker" Cathy Bryant models sleeveless 100% cotton knit mustard-colored T-dress. Size 22/24W. All-out impact when a curvy figure flows into a vertical-line dress. It's the knit fabric that "gives" to accommodate the curves! Photo credit: Linda Kanzinger.

(right) "Rulebreaker" Linda Kanzinger in a real shape definer, a pull-over shirt made from purple lightweight cotton gauze. Size Large. Worn with a purple cotton shirtwaist shirt. Size Large. Guess what her favorite color is! Photo credit: Erik Jonas.

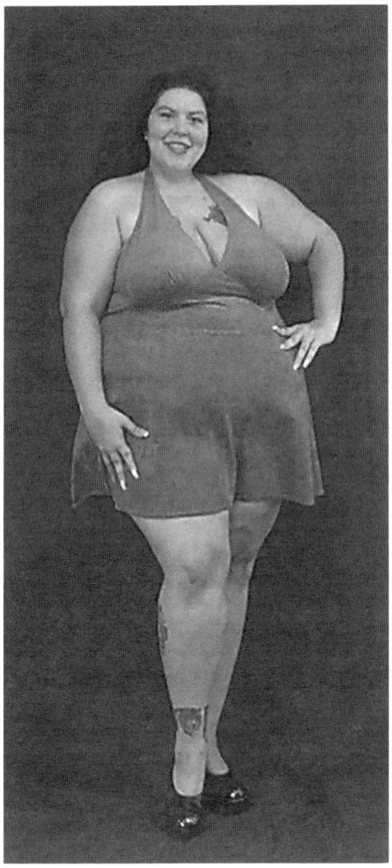

Hot stuff! Strut your stuff and go out on the town, hit the clubs!—in this close-fitting olive green suede halter dress, size 26/28W, with platform shoes. The cross-over V shape of the halter bodice and the A-line shape of the skirt enhances model Cleacia Foster's SuperVenus shape. Photo credit: Skip Orlando.

A flirty pose from Cathy Bryant in a white sweatshirt and maroon sweat pants while she's out jogging. Who says exercise can't be fun! Photo credit: Linda Kanzinger.

FOR A LARGE ABDOMEN OR STOMACH

No loose pleats
No gathered full skirts
No straight skirts
No gored skirts
No clingy fabrics
No tight waistbands
No bulky dirndls
No fabric that hang heavy
over the stomach
No tight belts

FOR BIG HIPS

No straight skirts
No pleated skirts
No gathered skirts
No bias cut skirts
No bold print skirts
No front-pleated pants or skirts
No straight pants,
unless worn with a top,
jacket, or vest which
"hides" the tops of the hip
No pleated pants
No back pockets
No back zippers
No bias skirts
No pleated skirts
No horizontal stripes
No fitted jackets
No plaid fabrics
No shiny fabrics
No pocket detail
No below-the-waist detail
No emphasis on a small waist

BIG REAR END

No short vests
No clingy skirts
No shirts that tuck in the waist
No fitted jackets with straight skirt
No pants, especially stretch pants

FOR LARGE THIGHS, HEAVY CALVES, THICK ANKLES

No knits
No knickers, jodhpurs
No pedal pushers or clam-diggers
No walking shorts

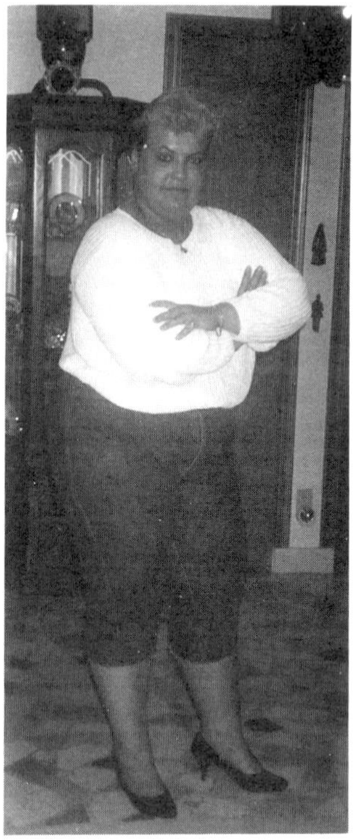

Gabby Sparapani's thinking—hard—while posing in this Betty Barclay designer yellow 100% cotton sweater with jeans, size 24W. Is she thinking that she might be breaking a rule of fashion, such as wearing pedal pushers with a focal point at the wide part of the calf?

"The importance to big women of feeling great in our clothes is something that cannot be overestimated. We live in a visual society"

Nancy Roberts -*Breaking All the Rules*

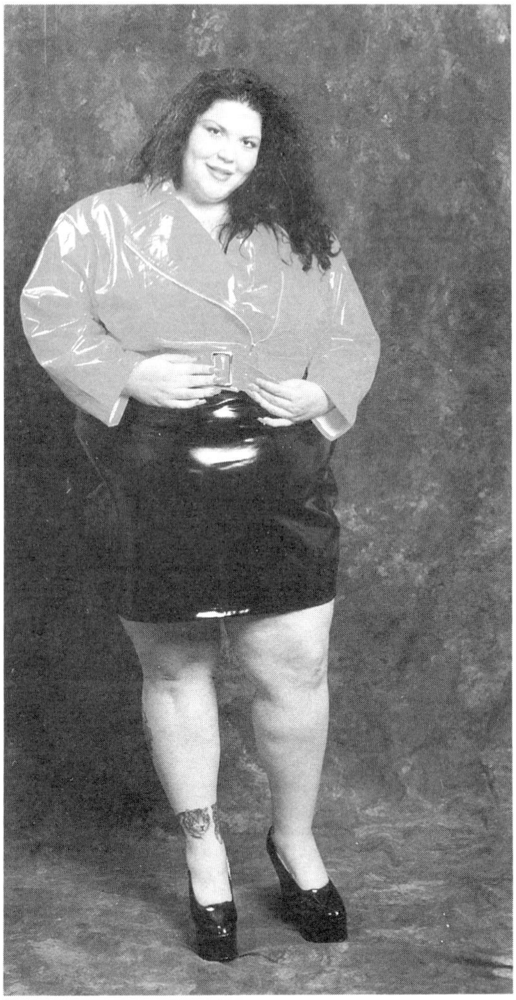

CLeacia Foster looks Reubenesquely "hot" in her red PVC jacket, from Barb's Large and Lovely, size 4X, along with a black PVC miniskirt, size 5X, from Love Your Peaches. Shiny black platform shoes complete the outfit. Photo credit: Skip Orlando.

TRADITIONAL "DO" RULES FOR "FIGURE FAULTS"

These rules have both do's and don'ts. Sometimes I think the do's are just camouflaged don'ts. See what you think!

FOR LARGE-FRAMED, FULL-FIGURED WOMEN

Do wear things that are well-fitted
Do wear clothes that are comfortably loose in the shoulder
Do wear jackets without lapels
Do wear V-neck sweaters
Do wear skirts with a slight flare
Do wear vertical lines

FOR WIDE, BROAD, AND SQUARE SHOULDERS

Do wear raglan shoulders and sleeves
Do wear dropped shoulders
Do wear unconstructed jackets
Do wear V-necks
Do wear diagonal interest at the pocket
Do wear diagonal interest at the hipline

FOR HEAVY ARMS

Do wear a long sleeve rolled up when others are wearing sleeveless
Do wear very long or very short sleeves
Do wear raglan sleeves
Do wear dolman sleeves
Do wear kimono sleeves
Do wear sleeves with a long unbroken line, no cuffs, and wide armhole cuts.

FOR LARGE BUST

Do wear V-necks
Do wear pretty colors and colors that flatter, leading up to the face
Do wear dark colors on the top, light on the bottom
Do wear raglan and dolman sleeves with fullness
Do wear monochromatic outfits
Do wear roomy simple designs

(Above) Ashley Taylor Clayton models a lovely lacy romantic purple dress from La Reina Boutique, Inc. Stretch satin bodice with charmeuse and chiffon skirt with Venice lace sleeves, bodice 100% silk. Size 22. Photo credit: Satu. (below) Liza Joy looks classic and sexy in a leopard print scoop-neck velvet top, Auchy fabric 69% acetate/20% nylon, 11% spandex. Size 16. Photo credit: Yan Dollar.

FOR A SMALL BUST

Do wear blouson blouses
Do wear A-line skirts

FOR A LARGE OR THICK WAIST

Do wear blouson waists
Do wear loose sheaths
Do wear drop waists
Do wear dresses with bloused backs
Do wear Chanel-type jackets
Do wear belts that drape around the hip area
Do wear a narrow belt the same color as the outfit

SHORT WAIST

Do wear blouson tops
Do wear tunic tops
Do wear tops outside(ie not tucked in)
Do wear loose layers
Do wear narrow waistbands that sit below the waist
Do wear monotone or close tone colors
Do wear ruffle neck blouses
Do wear scarves at the neck (to draw the eye upwards)

(upper right) Flaunting her style in an empire waist crinkle rayon print fabric, Myra Turley flirts with her fan. Tropical print with yellow cream background and hot tropical colors. Size 5. Photo credit: Linda Kanzinger.

"Rulebreaker" Andrea Hall shows that a big girl can sexily wear a silky sheath dress! Scoop neck orange-yellow 100% rayon sheath dress with maroon and deep red flower print. Size 26/28W. Once again, a straight-line dress flows easily over the curves of a big woman when fabric and design work together. The curved lines and rounded flower shapes of the print parallel the body shape, thus off-setting the straight line of the sheath dress, while the lightweightness and flexibility of the rayon fabric allows a straight-line design to lay lightly on a rounded body. Photo credit: Linda Kanzinger.

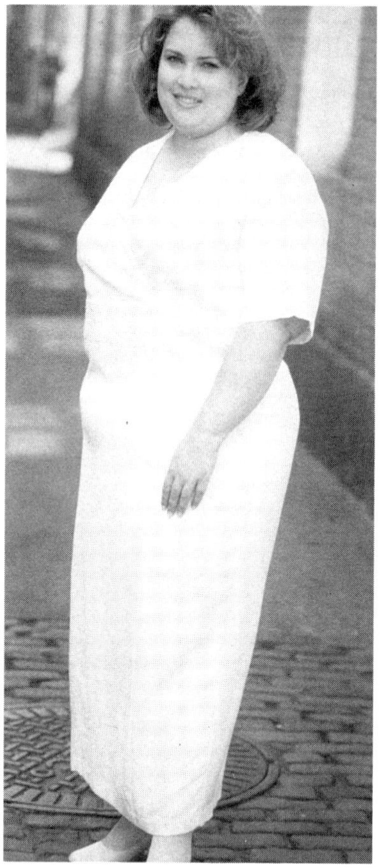

(right) This straight line V-neck empire style (with band) ankle length dress shows just a hint of belly, a comforting touch. Ivory rayon/acetate blend, size 20W Kelly Ryan models. Photo credit: Ignacio Rivas at Jim Woosley Photography, Mpls, MN.

FOR A LARGE ABDOMEN OR STOMACH

Do wear tunics
Do wear chemises
Do wear overblouses
Do wear waistless dresses
Do wear A-line skirts
Do wear skirts with
stitched down pleats
Do wear pleated skirts
(to 4 1/2 " pleats)
Do wear trousers with pleats
Do wear tiny floral prints
Do wear hard-finish fabrics

FOR BIG HIPS

Do wear A-line skirts
Do wear slightly gathered dirndls
Do wear an overblouse, top, jacket,
or vest which covers the top of the hips
Do wear box jackets
Do wear a broad shoulder line
Do wear vertical lines
Do wear slightly flared skirts
Do wear dark skirts with lighter tops
Do wear pants with unbuttoned jackets

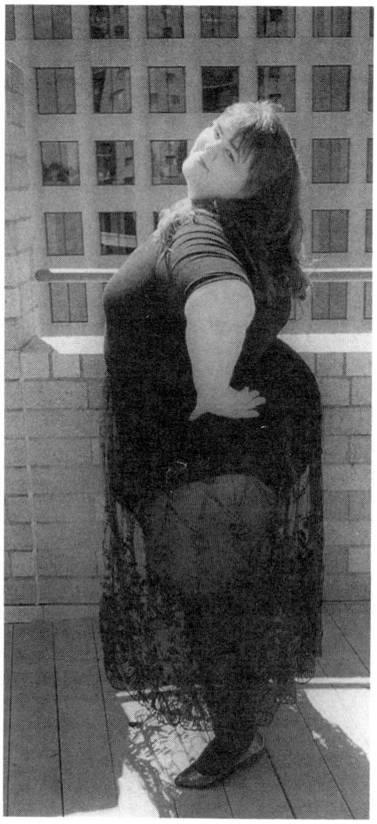

Taunting, or flaunting??? Cat Nordling reveals shape and substance in a black cotton/lycra jersey thong unitard! Over that she's wearing a black, beaded and sequined lace skirt from nylon fabric with elastic waistband, size 4X from The Great Changes Boutique (LA) . Photo credit: Peter Gujer.

BIG REAR END

Do wear long vests
Do wear caftans (the old hiding principle)
Do layering over pants
Do wear dirndl and pleated skirts
Do wear clothing that floats from
the arms and shoulders

FOR LARGE THIGHS, HEAVY CALVES, THICK ANKLES

Do wear tailored jumpsuits
with straight leg
Do wear pants with fuller cut
in a heavy nonclinging fabric

And the most popular rule of all, written in every fashion book, over and over and over:

> **"Do wear color at the neck to draw the attention to the face, to bring attention to your beautiful smile and wonderful personality"**
>
> **"Is this the 'Don't Look Rule': If I don't look below the neck, maybe there really won't be a big woman standing there?"**

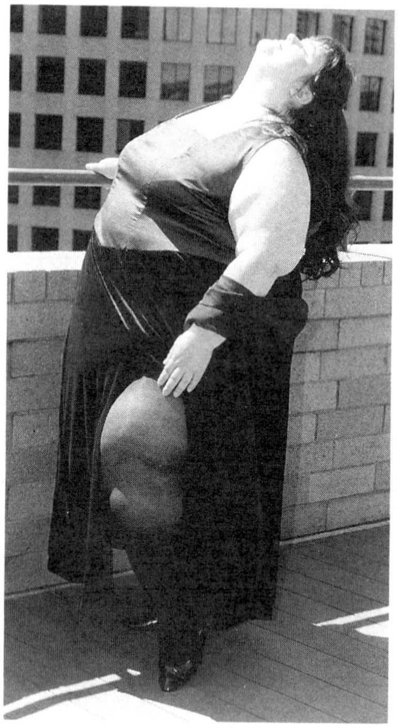

Exuberance exudes from this square necked plum-colored poly/satin and rayon/lycra stretch velvet dress with drape attachment and split skirt, designed and modeled by Cat Nordling! Thigh high slits follow the princess seam lines of the skirt and bodice. Drape yourself in the black chiffon shawl for extra enhancement! From size 32 sewing pattern. Photo credit: Staci Gilbert.

(above) Cheryl Anderson wants you to know she's hot stuff— in her straw hat, orange sling-back flats, white nylons, rayon flower-print jumper of many colors, gourd purse from Trinidad, and matching lipstick to boot! She also enjoys life enough to stop and smell the roses. Photo credit: John L. Smith.

(Below) A romantic look of Reubenesque proportions! Sharon Klose wears a lovely white dress with lace lined bodice; underlying dress of 100% rayon. Full swing 100% chiffon skirt added. From Another Thyme, size 34W. Photo credit: Perri Neri.

It is very easy to see that these rules are simply oppressive, a way to try and shame abundant women, keep them down, keep them in the house, keep them off balance, anxious, wondering what to wear, constantly trying to hide their body size and shape via all these contradictions.

IT IS OPPRESSIVE LANGUAGE.

IT IS THE LANGUAGE OF THE HOLDERS OF POWER TOWARD THOSE THEY SEE AS THEIR SUBJECTS—LESS THAN THEM.

IT IS THE LANGUAGE OF THE THIN AND MEDIUM SIZED (IE AVERAGE NORMAL OK) TOWARDS THE FAT. IT IS THE

LANGUAGE OF OPPRESSION.

OTHER PROBLEMS WITH THE RULES

For one thing, it gives the impression that a person has isolated body parts; that each part can be "fixed", rather than seeing your body as a whole. Also, full-bodied women have so many of the so-called "figure problems " that many of the rules cancel each other out; what works well for a large waist, for example, is counterproductive for a large abdomen, etc. Taking myself as an example, with large breasts, wide shoulders, large muscular upper arms, a protruding abdomen, and a subsiding-but-still-there hourglass figure; if I were to follow these rules, I would be hopelessly confused.The message I receive from this information is:

"... my body is not OK."

You can go crazy—and feel terrible about yourself and the prospect of buying clothes and building a wardrobe—trying to literally follow these rules. For example, for a large abdomen, it is suggest to wear high waistbands. This works by itself, but many large women who have large abdomens also have large "other parts", such as large breasts, and many women with this shape are also short-waisted. High waistbands are among the "Don'ts" for short waists and large breasts.

CRAZYMAKING MESSAGES

Think of some of the rules you read on the previous pages that are prevalent in most all fashion books. Messages such as "no tight clothes, no short skirts" send the message: "oh, m'god, how dare we think we're showing our body!!" The same fashion writers, however, encourage us to take advantage of our "presence" and to "not hide". Busty women in particular are encouraged to pretend they have no breasts. They are encouraged to wear boxy styles, minimizer bras, and the ultimate insult: get a breast reduction! Women with thick waists and large hips are told to wear an overjacket or vest to "hide" the waist and the top of the hips. Isn't this the "matronly look" that full-figured women have tried to hide in for centuries?

The Rules are especially onerous when they emphasize how the phat woman is denied rights that others assume. Something as basic as wearing sleeveless outfits when it is hot is denied by The Rules, and instead we are slapped in the face with advice such as "wear long sleeves rolled up when others wear sleeveless! " Now this really helps my self-esteem. The advice gets real bleak, with fat women told to wear dark solid pants with a long hip length cape. Talk about sending the message: "this body is ugly and must be covered!" They like to cover the bigness of the body with dark cloth. Big bust? Wear a dark top. Big bottom? Wear dark. What fashion-exciting advice! This is really going to encourage fat women to become fashion forward, isn't it?

Another crazy-making aspect of these rules is that the rules work for one body part, but not for another. A full stomach gets the go-ahead for front-pleated pants, but, oops, if you've got big hips as well, forget it! Are you small-busted with big hips—the typical Pear shape? You get the go-ahead for the A-line skirt on the bottom, but, oops, can't wear that blouson blouse that is recommended for the small bust. It will give you some "below the waist detail". Well, I guess you could just go ahead, follow The Rules, and just wear the A-line skirt. That would really turn heads.

Well, I hope you get my point from all the sarcastic comments I've made about The Rules. Just writing about it gives my head a cramp!

> "I'M OF THE STRONG OPINION THAT PHAT WOMEN SHOULD SHOW THEIR FIGURES MORE, RATHER THAN HIDING THEM IN LOOSE CLOTHING AND SHAME."

MY RULES!

OK— it's my turn. Everyone else has presented their rules, so here are mine.

> 1. WEAR ANYTHING YOU WANT!
> 2. FEEL GOOD IN WHAT YOU WEAR!
> 3. BARE SOME SKIN NOW AND THEN. (DO IT IN INCREMENTS IF IT MAKES YOU UNCOMFORTABLE)

CAN THE RULES BE OF ANY HELP?

I personally think that The Rules could be useful for plus-size designers, but they are definitely not helpful to plus-size consumers. The following is a sewing and designing principle which I learned from reading the book, *How To Make Sewing Patterns* by Donald McCunn. For example, one Rule says to wear loose layers if you are short waisted. I have seen very attractive plus-size clothing designs which are layered and flowing. The plus-size designer can start with a rule and "test" it. It then is a design idea, or suggestion. It is not an imposed constricting rule that consumers must follow. If the clothing designer tests the rule and designs an attractive piece of clothing, then the rule can be seen as utilitarian, rather than a moral judgment.

NOWHERE TO HIDE

I suggest that you use these rules as a crutch, and, as you feel better about your body, you can "throw away" the crutches, and reverse the negative thinking that says that you have to look at your curvaceous body as "something to hide".

> **"Piece by piece, you can 'come out', test the waters, and gradually throw away the 'thinking' of the Rules."**

IMPECCABLY DRESSED

Unfortunately, I see the old Rules being replaced in some cases by new ones. These new impositions focus on being "impeccably groomed". This is simply another admonition that fat women don't have the rights that average size women take for granted. When you are gardening or house-painting, you may not look **"impeccably groomed".**

Many fashion writers admonish the plus and supersize woman that she must, at all times, be immaculate, with clean, fashionably styled hair, well-groomed nails, and neatly pressed clothing. Of course, this is a reaction to the stereotype that fat women are dirty, lazy, or sloppy.

Are we responsible for a stereotype? I don't think so!

CONCLUSIONS

"I HOPE THAT, LIKE ME, YOU HAVE REACHED THE POINT WHERE THIS KIND OF ADVICE MAKES YOU ANGRY. IF WE WERE TO FOLLOW ALL THE GUIDELINES LAID DOWN BY SO-CALLED FASHION EXPERTS, WE'D BE LEFT WITH ABSOLUTELY NOTHING TO WEAR."

Nancy Roberts, *Breaking All the Rules*

My personal advice about The Rules is: use them wisely. Try them out. Some of them can work, and many don't work. Once you are aware of your specific body shape, it is a lot easier to apply the ones that do work, and cast out the rest. For example, as a Venus, I found that the rule of pleated pants is a good one for me. However, the rule that says no belts and no tight sweaters—well I haven't followed that advice for years! Decide which parts of your body you like best, and which you like second best. Then you can decide which to emphasize and which to de-emphasize.

> **"Try them out, see which ones work best for you, and throw out the rest. But see them only as techniques; they are not a morality."**

It is interesting to look at The Rules versus the philosophy in *The Triumph of Individual Style.*. With The Rules, all there is a long list of Don'ts for our various body parts. It becomes a very long list, and if one believed it to be "the Truth" it's no wonder they only dressed in black! No large prints. No stripes. I have found, in writing this book, that the more I look at plus and supersize women, the more diversity I see.

> **"And, the more I look at large women, the more I start liking womanly bodies: flesh, curves, roundness, jiggles."**

We as women have women's sized and shaped bodies for good reasons! And the more I move away from the (often unconscious) brainwashing that has us perceiving that the only beautiful women are the ones with the "ideal" (or approaching the ideal) figure, the more beautiful women I see. Ones with heavy bodies, curvy bodies, fat bodies. And many many different kinds of bodies. That is the uniqueness, and the richness, of life!

> **"There are all kinds of women's bodies. Let us promote tolerance of diversity of women's bodies."**

"REMEMBER THAT PEOPLE IN OTHER CULTURES CELEBRATE BIGNESS MORE THAN DOES AMERICAN CULTURE. AMERICAN CULTURE HAS DOWNSIZED WHICH BODY SIZE IS ACCEPTABLE."

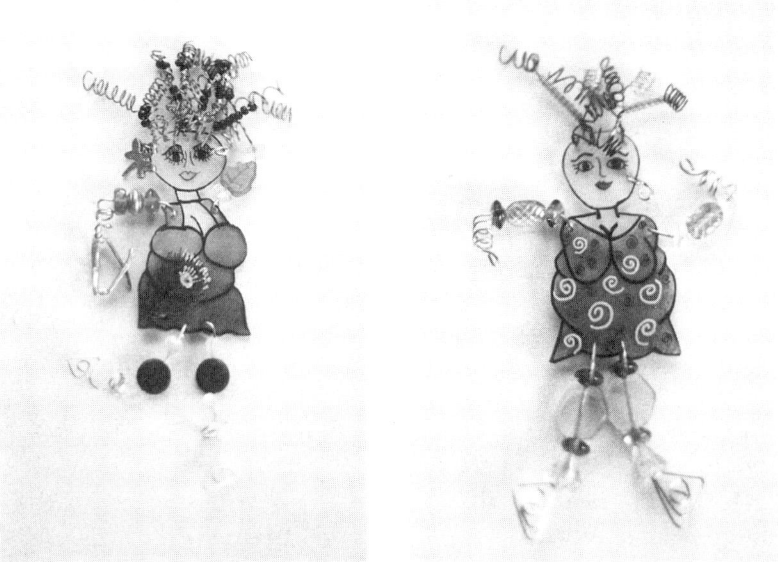

(left) Kim Caldwell's "Diva dolls" made from PolyShrink plastic, rubber stamps, wire, and beads. "Red Lady" 3" x 5 1/2". "Purple Lady" 3" x 5". © 1999 by Kim Caldwell on both. Photo credit: Linda Kanzinger.

5

BASIC SHAPES OF PLUS AND SUPERSIZE WOMEN

"CLOTHES CAN BE DESIGNED FOR BODIES, RATHER THAN BODIES DESIGNED FOR CLOTHES."

Linda Kanzinger- *Size-Positive Style!*

"WE ARE WOMEN OF DIMENSION. WE ARE SCULPTURES. WE AREN'T FLAT PAPER DOLL CUTOUTS."

Linda Kanzinger- *Size-Positive Style!*

Now that we've all agreed on how unique we are and how we can dress in a creative way by accepting the bodies we have, I'd like to loosely outline for you a typology, or a system of categorization, of different types of curvy women's bodies. Why is this important? I think it is important in that all zoftig women are not shaped the same. It will be easier to find clothing styles in the stores that work best for your body type when you have an idea of what type of body shape you have! For those of you who sew, it will be much easier to have this basic understanding of your shape before designing clothes for yourself, or someone else.

This is one of the distinctive things that I want to do in this book—to provide a way for you to identify just which general shape you are, so that you can choose attractive clothing more easily, rather than by the hit-and-miss method.

BODY TYPES

A number of articles in women's magazines have emphasized body types in choosing clothing. They mention shapes such as:

- **Pear-shaped**
- **Round**
- **Rectangular**
- **Square**

From this, a person can then figure out which types of clothing look best on them. How is this beneficial in understanding the various big body shapes of plus and supersized women? I feel it is helpful, especially visually, in looking at large shapes, and seeing the underlying basic geometrical shapes that comprise our figures. There are also a number of correlations between the various typologies (mine and other's).

GENERAL SHAPES

First there is the older anthropological view of body types: with

- the **Ectomorph**
  with no visible muscle or fat;
- the **Mesomorph**
  of medium build, visible muscle, bone, but not much visible fat, and usually has broad shoulders and narrow hips.
- the **Endomorph**
  rounded, heavily built, the middle section is thick, and muscles are firm.

Doris Poosner , author of *Always in Style,* formed a body typology that is linked to dressing well. Her typology is not written for abundant women, but I find its concepts to be useful.

She describes a continuum of body shapes, based on simple shapes: from the triangle through the square and rectangle to the ellipse, oval and circle. First, she delineates two basic categories: **straight-line body types and rounded body types. Straight-line body types** are usually:

- tall
- broad shoulders
- small hips or flat hips
- small busts
- square, rectangular bodies

Whereas **rounded body types** have:

- full bust
- curved hips
- shaped waists
- soft, smooth curves

These are her further delineations:

Straight-line Body Shape

Sharpstraight
- diamond or square face
- broad shoulders
- straight, squarish torso

Straight
- squarish face
- square or rectangular body

Mixed Body Shape

Soft-straight
- oval face
- rectangular body

Rounded Body Shape

Soft-curved
- oval face
- curved body

Curved
- round face
- very curved, voluptuous body

When you look at the following body shapes, you will be able to more clearly see the underlying basic geometrical shapes—the circle, the triangle, the rectangle, and the X or double triangle, that comprise our figures.

To really study the shapes of bodies and the shapes within bodies, I also recommend that you read *The Triumph of Individual Style* by Carla Mason Mathis and Helen Villa Connor.

But first, more of other people's ideas on body shapes!

GENERAL FASHION BOOKS

General fashion books (as opposed to specific plus-size fashion books) have also codified typologies. In the book, *Womanstyle*, Leah Feldon offers:

- **Renoir**
- **Athlete**
- **Pear**
- **the Bulge**

In a following title, *Dress Like a Million*, her categories are:

- **Rose**
- **Tulip**
- **Lily**
- **Orchid**

Barbara Weiland, in *Clothes Sense*, describes:

- **Hourglass**
- **Triangle**
- **Inverted Triangle**
- **Rectangle**

In the book *Metamorphosis*, author David Kibbe describes what his image-identity body types look like if they are overweight.

Mary Martin Niepold, author of *Overnight Guide to Dressing Thin*, describes four different body types:

- **Straight up and down**
- **Top-heavy**
- **Bottom-heavy**
- **Hourglass**

In the book *Uniquely You*, Betty Nethery and Beverly Bush Smith describe the following five shapes:

A or Pear shape: narrow shoulders, wider hips
H-V shape: straight up and down
Perfect Shape: The Ideal Body Shape
T-shape: big in the thighs
X-shape: Hour glass; has a well-defined waist; gains weight all over

This is the general consensus for body types in both mainstream fashion books as well as books on plus size fashion.

PLUS SIZE FASHION BOOKS

Plus-size fashion books also have categorizations of large size bodies. In *Sewing for Plus Sizes*, Barbara Deckert uses :

- **Apple**
- **Pear**
- **Potato**
- **Supersized (generally a Potato)**
- **Madame Peanut**

In Plus *Style*-Suzan Nanfeldt includes:

- **Apple**
- **Pear**
- **Hourglass**
- **Rectangle**

Rita Farro, in *Life is not a Dress Size*, has:

- **Ruby Reubenesque**
- **Winona Wineglass**
- **Christina Christmas Tree**

In *Style is not a Size*, Hara Marano offers:

- **Square**
- **Pear**
- **Hourglass**
- **Barrel**

In *Fashion Design for the Plus-Size*, Frances Leto Zangrillo offers

- **Rectangular-8 Shape**
- **Pear shape**
- **Barrel Shape**
- **Box Shape**

The Lane Bryant Fashion Math Make-Over uses:

- **Triangle**
- **Rectangle**
- **Diamond**
- **Circle**

Ann Harper, in *The Big Beauty Book*, has:

- **Figure 8**
- **Pear Shape**
- **Barrel Shape**
- **Box Shape**

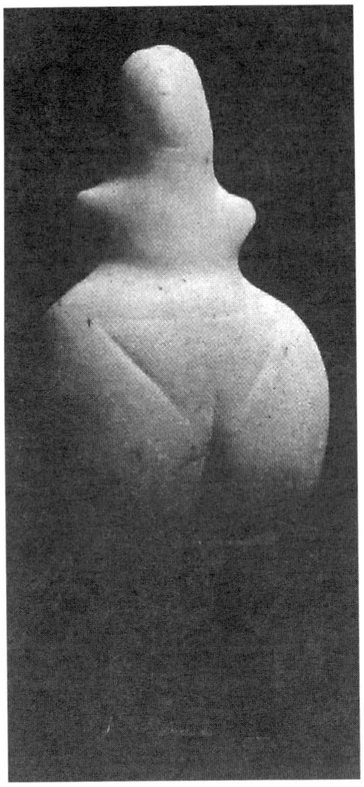

Example of the familiar Pear shape: "Pear shaped goddess figure." White marble figurine. Tell Azmak, central Bulgaria. Early sixth millennium BC. Photo credit: Historical Museum of Stara Zagora, Bulgaria.

Example of the Apple shape: "Fat Lady of Sitagroi", Macedonia. East Balkan civilization. c. 4500 BC. Photo credit: Philipi Museum, Greece.

THE FOUR BASIC TYPES AS DESCRIBED IN MOST ALL FASHION BOOKS: THE PEAR SHAPED FIGURE, THE APPLE SHAPED FIGURE, THE BOX OR RECTANGULAR SHAPED FIGURE, AND THE X-SHAPED FIGURE.

"Seated nude figurine from Thessaly" Sesklo culture, 6000 BC. Squarish lines define this mostly Rectangular figure. Photo credit: National Museum Belgrade.

This Goddess figure clearly has a curvy shape with a clearly defined waist, thus exemplifying the X-shaped figure. "Goddess, Terra Cotta, Mesopotamia, c. XXIV century BC. Photo Credit: Louvre Museum, Paris, France.

I. SQUARE OR ROUND

The first variable I see is: **square or round.**

Some of us are more muscular with big bone structure. This causes us to have more squarish shapes, regardless of how much fat overlays the bone and muscle. People with dominant bone and muscle in their bodies are going to have squarish silhouettes.

These are given various names such as **box, square, H, rectangular, etc.**

Others of us are small or medium-boned, without much developed musculature. Thus, our bodies appear more round.

This body type is called: **Barrel, O, Pear, Renoir, A,** by various writers.

GAUGUIN, Paul.
The Moon and the Earth {Hina Te fatou}. 1893.
Oil on burlap, 45 x 24 1/2" (114.3 x 62.2 cm).
The Museum of Modern Art, New York. Lillie P. Bliss Collection.
Photograph © 2000 The Museum of Modern Art, New York.

Note the squarish lines of the body in the thick calves and feet.

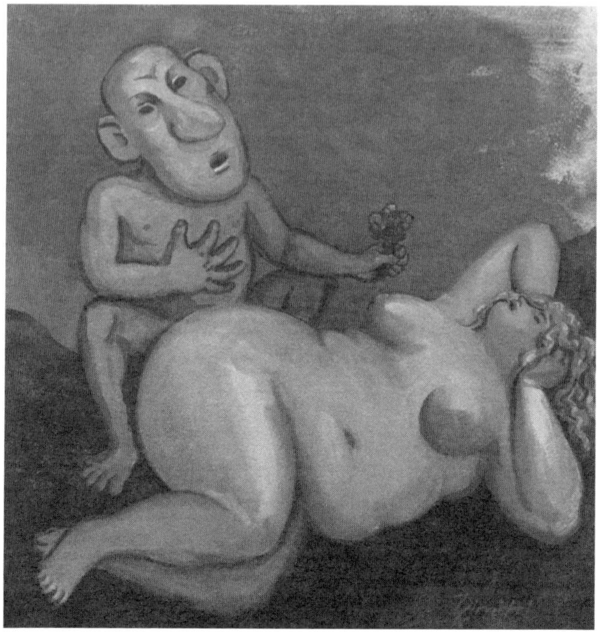

"The Barbarian Goddess"- Dimitri Kare. Gouache on watercolor paper. 13" x 13". The rounded curves of the woman's body are eloquently depicted in this painting. © Dimitri Kare.

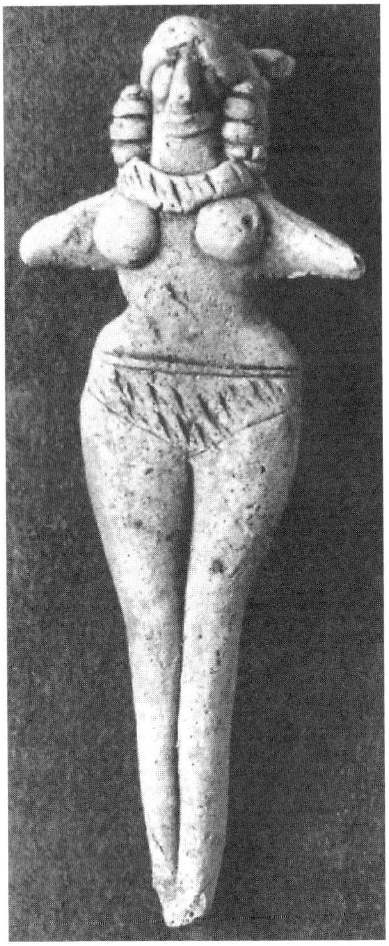

(right) ."Goddess, Terra Cotta, Mesopotamia, has a clearly defined waist. c. XXIV century BC. Photo Credit: Louvre Museum, Paris, France.

III. TONED OR NOT TONED:FIRM FAT OR FAT THAT MOVES

The next variable I see is how toned we are. (See below) Some of us have probably been told "You carry your weight well". Some fat is firm; some fat is flabby. Regardless of how much body fat we have, toned muscles are more of a support for the layers of fat than untoned. Some of my distinctions in large women's body shapes comes from the amount of firmness in the flesh.

II. WAIST OR NO WAIST

The second variable I see is: **Waist or no waist.** (See above)

Some of us plus-size types have well-defined waists, whether we weigh 175, 225, or 350 lbs. With a waist, we are going to have some kind of an "X" shape, rather than an actual square or round shape.

This shape can be called: **Pear, Hourglass, X, Figure-8, A, etc.**

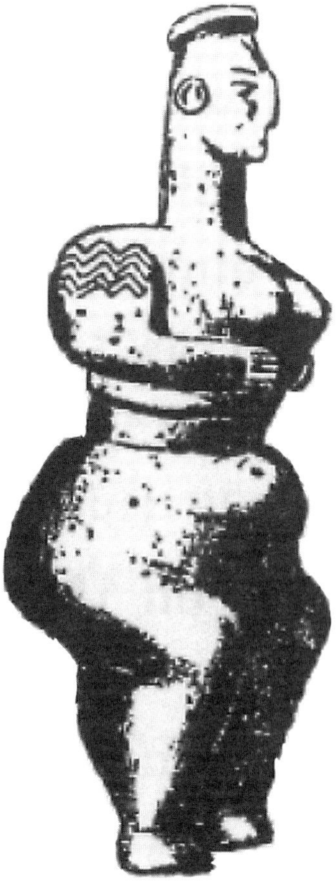

(left) This figure appears quite solid even with big belly, hips, and thighs. "Island Figure". Limestone, near Sparta. c.xv century(?)BC. From *The Great Mother*- Erich Neumann. Photo credit: M Hornes, Urgeschichte der bildenden Kunst in Europa. Wien; Schroll (1925) p 60 Fig 9. Deutsches Archaologisches Institut, Berlin, Germany.

Example of a tall Venus-shaped woman. "Sitting Nude" - T'Rina Headlee. Even though she is in a sitting position, you can tell how tall, voluptuous, and shapely she is! Prismacolor pencil drawing. © 1999 by T'Rina Headlee.

IV. LENGTH AND TALLNESS

If you are 5'8" and weigh 275 lbs, you are going to have a different shape than if you are 5' 3" and weigh 275 lbs. In both of these examples, the women are big, but the proportions of the figure are going to change based upon the height of the body. The height, ie the length, of the figure, changes the overall distribution of fat.

As well, some of us are short-waisted, some are of average waist length, while others are long-waisted. This is going to affect our general body shape as well.

V. RATIO OF BODY FAT TO BONE AND MUSCLE

Your shape is going to be partially dependent upon how much body fat you carry in relation to how big your bone structure is and your musculature. Your weight by number doesn't make a distinction between these three factors, so that three different people could all weigh 225 lbs, and yet have different body shapes due to person A carrying more body fat, person B being tall with a large bone structure, and person C being short but with large muscles as well as a fair amount of body fat.

These are the basic underlying features that I see that differentiate full-figured women's body types. Below is my more specific typology. It is based up the visual observation of countless numbers of plus and supersize women, plus information gathered from a questionnaire distributed across the country to fat women. Our differing body shapes affect how clothes fit us, and what types of clothes flatter us. Depending on our shapes, we can wear certain styles of clothing more successfully.

(below) "The Fat Lady of Sitagroi" exemplifies a short, squat figure. Macedonia. East Balkan civilization. c. 4500 BC. Photo credit: Philipi Museum.

SHAPES OF PLUS SIZE WOMEN

PEAR: a common and familiar shape among all women.

Small frame (bone structure) and build
Sloping shoulders
Small bust
Average sized waist
Large hips
Large derriere, often protruding as well (wide and deep!)
Heavy thighs, calves
can be short, medium, or tall

OUTSTANDING FEATURE: derriere is pear shaped, with a much smaller upper body and waistline.

The Pear shape is quite familiar. Average-size women, as well as plus-size women, often become pear-shaped. In the Pear body shape, the lower body is much larger than the upper body. Often the upper body is quite small: sloping shoulders, small breasts, and a defined waist. Once moving down from the waist, the hips widen, the stomach is large, the thighs are large, and the rear is large and wide, thus the name pear-shaped or Pear! Many average size women who are pear-shaped wear a size smaller on top, so if you are a size 16 or larger on top, it's likely that you are a Plus or Supersize Pear!

It's important when assessing your figure as a Pear to decide whether or not you are a large woman in the first place. You may be big on the bottom, but not truly fit into the plus-sizes.

CHECK ARTWORK : *"Tree of Death"* (German, 16th century woodcut).

CHECK GODDESS IMAGE: *"The Lady of Pazardzik"* (also known as the *Thrace Goddess*); *"Goddess, Clay, Cyprus,* c. 2500 BC.

Cathy Bryant works out by lifting weights. She's wearing a sports bra and bicycle shorts made of a cotton/lycra blend. Photo credit: Linda Kanzinger.

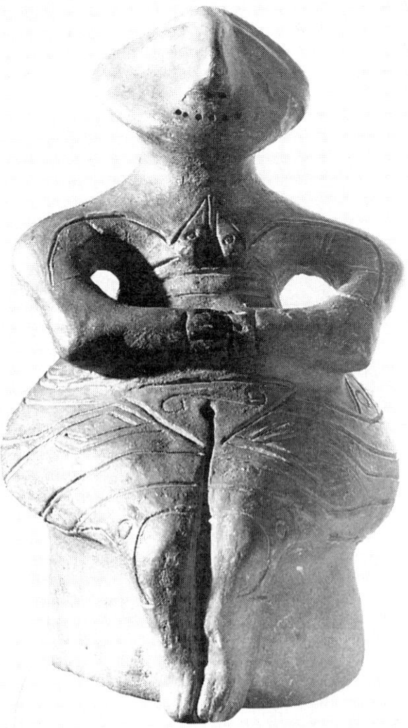

"The Lady of Pazardzik" , central Bulgaria, East Balkan civilization. c. 4500 BC. Photo credit: Naturhistorisches Museum Wien, Photo: Alice Schumacher.

(above) "Angel with Flowers" by Dimitri Kare. Stamp image from pen and ink drawing. © Dimitri Kare. (below) Cathy Bryant in workout outfit: black lycra/spandex sports bra and bicycle shorts with white stripe. Photo credit: Linda Kanzinger. She is an example of a Tall Reubenesque.

VENUS: So named for Venus de Milo, a curvy Greek.

Moderate bone structure or frame, with well-developed muscles
Heavy upper arms
Average width shoulders
Large to very large bust
Defined waist (hourglass)
Protruding stomach/abdomen
Rounded rear
Heavy thighs and calves
Approximately 5'5" to 5'7"
A curved silhouette

OUTSTANDING FEATURE: bosomy, with a defined waist.

Venus is also a familiar body type, named from the goddess of love with her curvy feminine features, well-defined bust, waist, and hips. Technically speaking, a Venus will have a bust and hips 10" or more than the size of the waist. A figure of 51" bust, 40" waist, and 50" hips is a Venus. A tip to distinguish between the Venus and the Reubenesque, who is also shapely and curvy is: does the bosom stand out in the overall figure? Then the woman is a Venus!

CHECK ARTWORK : *"Two Nudes, or the Bath "*- Suzanne Valadon; *"Diana"*-Pierre Auguste Renoir; *"Woman with a Mirror"*-Botero.

CHECK GODDESS IMAGE: *"Pillar Headed Goddess with Folded Arms."* Hamangia culture.

REUBENESQUE: After Peter Paul Reubens who painted voluptuous women.

Large bone structure with well-developed muscles
solidly built, stocky (firm fat)
Short in stature (5'0" to 5'4")
Heavy upper arms
Squarish shoulders
A defined waist
Large hips and thighs
Medium to large bosom
Fat/muscle ratio fairly equal
Usually weighs 200+ lbs
A squarish silhouette

OUTSTANDING FEATURES: Short, stocky, firm flesh, and curvy.

CHECK ARTWORK: *"The Baker's Wife"*- Edgar Degas.

CHECK GODDESS IMAGE: *"Woman with a child and a dog"* near Palenque, Mexico.

TALL REUBENESQUE: This type is a variation on the standard Reubenesque. She has similar features, except for the height.

Squarish shoulders and heavy upper arms
Shoulder width equal to hips
Large hips and thighs
Stocky, solidly built
Medium bust
Firm, solid , fat
Tall 5'7"-up
Weight usually 250 and up

OUTSTANDING FEATURE: Because of her height, and womanly features, she gets noticed!

CHECK ARTWORK: *"Nude with a Hat"*- Pierre Auguste Renoir.

CHECK GODDESS IMAGE: *"Seated nude figurine from Thessaly".* Sesklo culture.

RENOIR: named for the Renoir women that the artist painted, full-bodied, womanly.

Average frame
Soft tone, rather than muscular
Medium shoulders
Medium bust
Medium-heavy upper arm
Wide waist with a little curve
Protruding stomach
Fleshy hips
Very large thighs
Large calves
Medium height

OUTSTANDING FEATURE: What differentiates the Renoir is that the lines are fluid and curvy. Usually a Renoir does not have much developed muscle tone, she is soft rather than firm.

CHECK ARTWORK: *"Blond Bather"* and *"Ode to Flowers"*- Pierre Auguste Renoir.

An example of Tall Reubenesque: "Seated nude figurine from Thessaly" Sesklo culture, 6000 BC. Photo credit: National Museum Belgrade.

(above) An ideal image of the Renoir woman. "Blonde Bather "- Pierre-Auguste Renoir. 1881. Oil on canvas. "32 3/16" x 25 7/8". Photo credit: © Sterling and Francine Clark Art Institute, Williamstown, Massachusetts. (opposite page, top: Cathy Bryant begins her workout, wearing bicycle shorts with white stripe, sports bra, and black and white nylon jacket.

Apple shaped figure. "Fat Lady of Sitagroi", Macedonia. East Balkan civilization, c. 4500 BC. Photo credit: Philipi Museum, Athens, Greece.

APPLE: This shape is very similar to Reubenesque except the lines are rounded rather than squarish. This person has more body fat and less muscle than Reubenesque.

Small bone structure; weak musculature
Short in stature (4'8"-5'5")
Fat/muscle ratio: much more fat
Shoulders are sloped
Most weight carried on upper front of body
Bosom is small to medium
Waist and stomach merge
Abdomen is large
Upper arms are heavy
Hips and thighs are small to average
Legs and calves are slender

OUTSTANDING FEATURE: The middle of the body is very round; body fat is focused above the hipline on the front of the figure.

CHECK GODDESS IMAGE: *"Female Figurine,* Terra cotta, Peru, pre-Columbian"; *"Fat Lady of Sitagroi"*; *"The Maltese Goddess"* ca. 3600-3000 B.C.Limestone,Malta.

BOX OR RECTANGLE: This figure is similar to the Apple shape, but the lines are squarish rather than rounded.

Weight is carried above the waist
Average build
Average musculature
Large, heavy arms
Small-medium breasts (if large breasted a Reubenesque due to the curviness of the figure rather than "boxy")
No waist—straight up and down
Fat on shoulders and upper back
Average or small size derriere
Small thighs and calves, in comparison to rest of body
5'6" to 5'9" medium to tall in height

OUTSTANDING FEATURE: The figure is top-heavy in a squarish way while the lower body is smaller.

CHECK ARTWORK: *"Moon and the Earth"*and *"Spirit of the Dead Watching"*- Paul Gauguin.

CHECK GODDESS IMAGE: *"Classical Cucuteni Bird or Snake Goddess".*

SCALLOPED: With this body shape, the noticeable thing is that the fat is carried only on the front of the body.

Small, medium, or large bosom
Small to medium bone structure
Small or medium musculature
Defined waistline
Belly rolls forward into very large lower belly in "scallop" shape
Average sized hips, thighs, and legs

OUTSTANDING FEATURE: Weight falls only on the front of figure rather than on the front and back. When looking at this body shape from the side, you could draw a line between the front, rounded half, and the straight, back half.

CHECK ARTWORK: *"The Bathers"* - Pierre-Auguste Renoir.

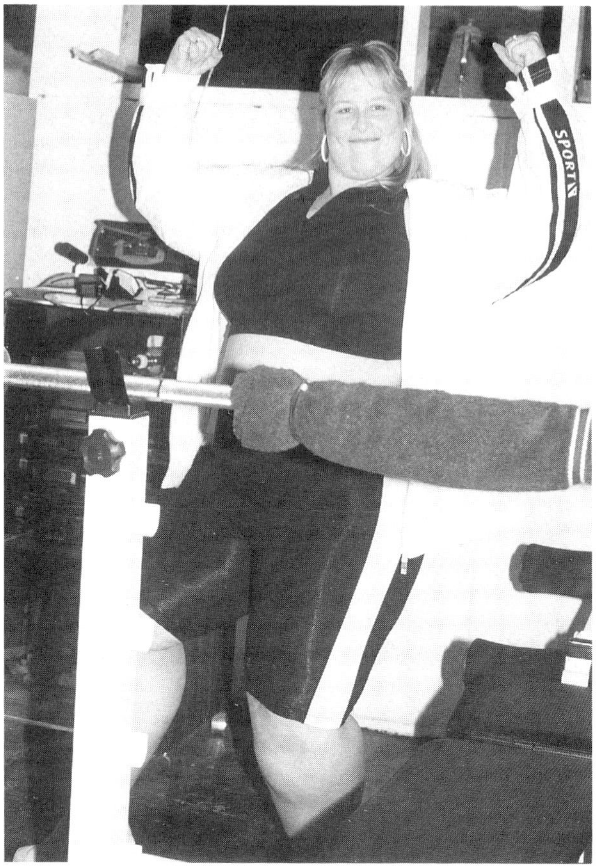

(above) Success! It pays to try. Cathy Bryant working out. Photo credit: Linda Kanzinger. (left) "Tag". Kim Caldwell. Rubber stamps, ribbon, ink. Stamps from Her Rubber. Reubenesque dancers and figures with stamped lettering. Photo credit: Linda Kanzinger.

(right) "The Bathers"- Pierre-Auguste Renoir. c. 1918-1919. Oil on canvas. 43 3/8" by 63". Gift of the artist's sons, 1923. Photo credit: Paris, Musee d'Orsay.

(above) Jeri Carmichael in a red long-sleeved 90% rayon/10% lycra dress with hip pleats, size 26/28W. The style of this dress both reveals the curves of the SuperPear's figure, as well as adding a romantic touch with the hip pleats.

(left) Jeri Carmichael models her black/shiny gold 2 piece bathing suit. 90% nylon, 10% lycra. Top: size 22/24W; bottom: size 26/28W. A gorgeous supersize woman!

SUPERSIZE SHAPES

THE LANDSCAPES OF THE SUPERSIZE BODY

As the body gains weight, the shapes are less defined, and can be seen more as landscape, sculpture, with deep crevasses, folds, and swaying movement of fat that swings. Weight accumulates in varying ways. Two supersize women of the same height and weight can have very different shapes.

Although its' variations may escape classification, I am attempting to capture the ripples and folds, and the magnificence, of the larger figure. Thus, I see the supersize body as a landscape, to be explored in all of its' nuance. For the purposes of designing and wearing clothes, and being successful in learning how to dress for ones' unique body, I am proposing the following classification.

As well, the supersize figure was not born that way, but moved through various stages, including plus-size. I have linked my supersize typology to the plus-sizes. As a woman gains more fat, the former plus-size shape metamorphoses into the supersize shape. This is how I have linked the shapes.

PLUS SIZE **Becomes**	SUPERSIZE
Apple	**Goddess**
Reubenesque	**Goddess**
Pear	**SuperPear**
Pear	**S-Shaped Woman**
Venus	**SuperVenus**
Tall Reubenesque	**SuperReubenesque**
Box or Rectangle	**SuperReubenesque**
Renoir	**Juno**
Scallop	**SuperScallop**

SUPERSIZE TYPOLOGY

SUPERPEAR: similar to the Pear shape, but supersized; a common and familiar shape.

Small -medium bone structure
Narrow sloping shoulders
Upper arms are bigger
Lower arm is average size
Small bust

Has a defined waist
Waist measurement is smaller than below waist
Big contrast between upper & lower body; Upper body is " average" sized while lower body is much bigger
Very large superbig hips
Superbig thighs
Superbig rear, often called " bottom-heavy" by admirers
Can be short, medium, or tall

OUTSTANDING FEATURE: Supersize Pear women are very rounded, especially below the waist.

CHECK ARTWORK: *"Venus on Green"*- Dimitri Kare; *"Apples and Pears"*- Dimitri Kare.

CHECK GODDESS IMAGE: Goddess reference: *"Sleeping Woman"*, Clay, Malta, neolithic.

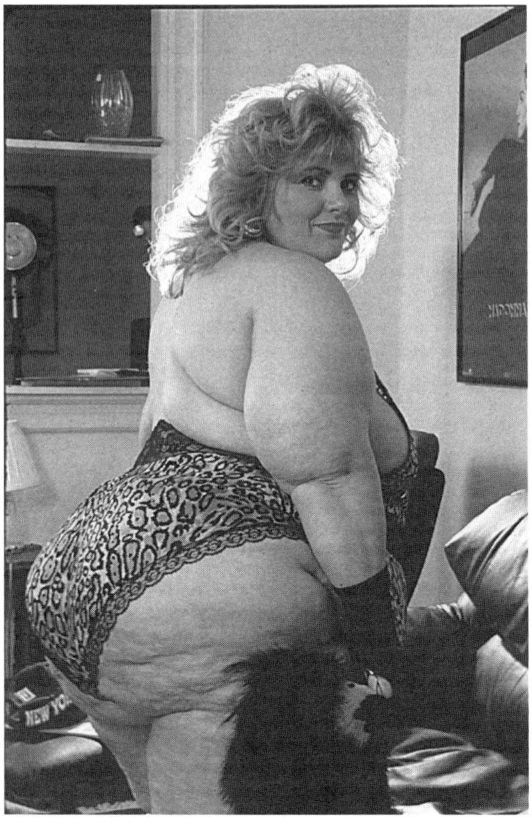

(above) Nancy Goddess in a leopard teddy with black feather boa and leather gloves. Photo credit: Lee Fegan Studios, Jersey City, NJ.

SUPERVENUS: A bigger Venus shape.

Squarish shoulders with heavy upper arms
Medium to large build
Muscular
Very large bust
Medium tall
Waist 10" less than bust or hips
Very wide and big hips,
Hips and bust approximately the same width across the figure
Big thighs
Big calves, but tapers to a slender ankle

OUTSTANDING FEATURE: very bosomy, with equally big hips, with a defined waist to balance the figure.

CHECK ARTWORK: *"Black Venus"*- Nikki De St. Phalle; *"Sitting Nude"*- T'Rina Headlee; *"Floating Figure"*- Gaston Lachaise.

CHECK GODDESS IMAGE: *"Dolni Vestonice".*

(lower right) In a purple bra, 44DD, and panties size 26/28. Cleacia Foster is an example of a SuperVenus! Photo credit: Skip Orlando.

GODDESS: Goddesses have bodies that are like the ancient Goddess figures, symbols of fertility and plenty.

They tend to be short, 5' or under
Body lines are rounded, not squarish
Bone structure is small to medium
Goddess bodies are blessed with much fatness
Bellies are very big
Musculature is hidden by abundant amounts of fat

OUTSTANDING FEATURE: A lot of fat is carried on a substantially short body.

CHECK ARTWORK: *"Woman Smoking a Cigarette"*- Botero.

CHECK GODDESS IMAGE: *"Venus of Willendorf"* (also called *"The Great Goddess of Willendorf"*).

Example of SuperVenus: "The Great Goddess of Willendorf" c. 25,000 BC. Photo credit: Naturhistorisches Museum, Vienna. Photo: Alice Schumacher.

SUPER REUBENESQUE: She is always tall. She is fatter than the Tall Reubenesque, but still is muscular and has a squarish build.

Squarish shoulders and heavy upper arms
Shoulder width equal to hips
Large hips and thighs
Stocky, solidly built
Medium bust
Firm, solid , fat
Big solid belly
Wide waist
Squarish figure
Tall 5'7"-up
Weight usually 350-500+

OUTSTANDING FEATURE: A woman of substance, SuperReubenesque is "all woman". She exemplifies bodacious bigness!

CHECK ARTWORK: *"Nude with a Hat"*- Renoir.

CHECK GODDESS IMAGE: *"Island Figure"*.

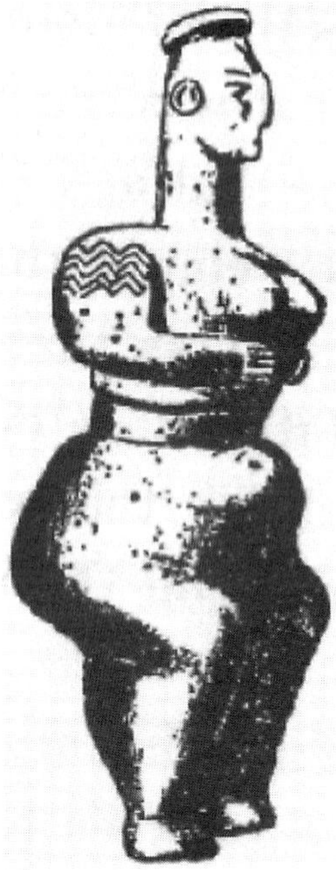

(above) An example of SuperReubenesque. "Island Figure" Limestone, near Sparta. c.xv century(?)BC. From *The Great Mother*- Erich Neumann. Photo credit: M Hornes, Urgeschichte der bildenden Kunst in Europa. Wien; Schroll (1925) p 60 Fig 9. Deutsches Archaologisches Institut, Berlin, Germany.

JUNO: big all over, and tall, but like a Renoir body type, a soft fat body with rounded lines, with little musculature to support it.

Usually tall, 5'7" and over
Bone structure is small or medium
"Big all over" with the exception of a small or medium bosom
Large upper arms,
Big waist,
Large hips,
Large belly
Thighs more fat, less muscle
Average size calves, not very muscular
Body weight slopes down
300-450 lb range

OUTSTANDING FEATURE: Named for the Greek goddess, Juno women are women of substance: tall and very big. Like the Renoir shape, they are also soft and cushiony rather than firm.

CHECK GODDESS IMAGE: *"Goddess of Laussel".*

CHECK ARTWORK: *" Staffeli Dame"*- Lis Gede.

SUPERSIZE SCALLOP: The fat accumulates primarily on the front of the body. Generally scalloping out from bosom through stomach to abdomen, the sideways silhouette is similar to a scalloped edge, or it could look like the letter B in a double formation.

Short, medium, or tall
Small build, not much musculature
Medium to large bosom
Belly is large
Hips are narrow
Rear end is flat
Thighs more fat, less muscle

OUTSTANDING FEATURE: Large amounts of fat are carried primarily on the front of the body.

CHECK ARTWORK: *"Vandkande Dame"*- Lis Gede.

These basic shapes are meant as general archetypal images, not representative of one particular woman. However, in doing research for this book, I observed many plus and supersize women and realized that we are multi-shaped, yet with characteristics which can be categorized.

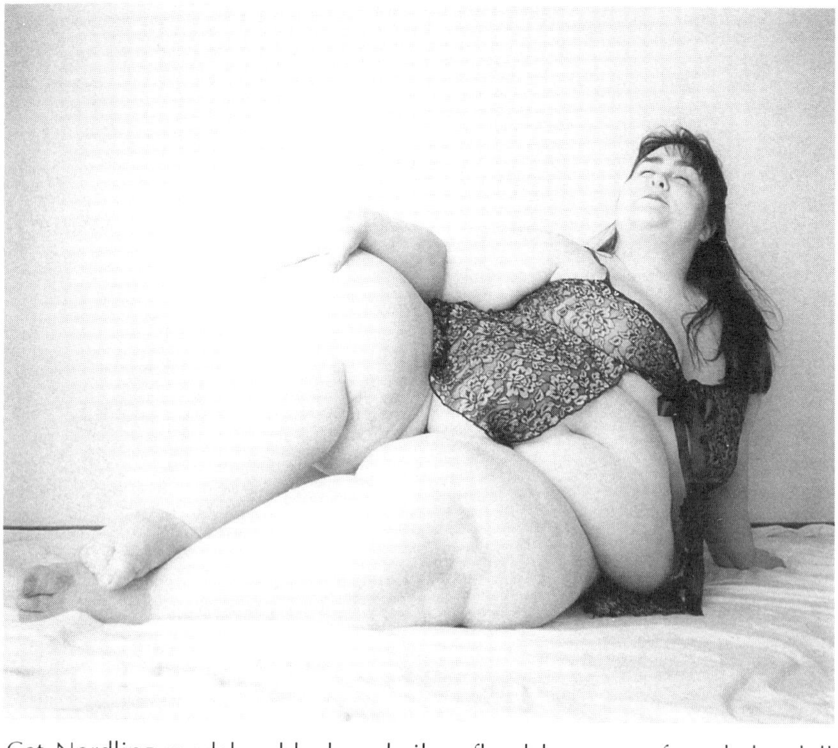

Cat Nordling models a black and silver floral lace open-front baby doll nightie with thong panties. 60% nylon, 40% rayon, size 26/28W. Photo credit: Peter Gujer.

MOTIFS

These next two descriptions, while not quite "types", still describe an outstanding feature of the figure that makes this body shape unique.

HEART-SHAPED WOMAN: This body shape has a dominant "heart" motif, either on the high hips, or on the upper thigh. In the one, the fat is on the upper thigh, otherwise known as having "saddlebag" hips.

In the other, the fat is on the upper hips—and the line drops into a heart-shaped shape. The rear is fairly flat. This woman is very curvy with very large, rounded hips. Because the high hip (2-3" below the waist) is where the fat accumulates, rather than the regular hip line (8' below the waist), the rear end from the back has a "heart-shape" design. Often the actual bottom is flat, rather than curved.

CHECK ARTWORK: *"The Lesson on Botony"*- Leonore Fini; *"Young Girls"*-Bruno Epple.

S-SHAPED WOMAN: There is an S shape from the belly around the hip and the rear end to the upper thigh . The belly is smooth, rounded. There is no line between the stomach and abdomen, unlike the Scalloped Shape Woman. If you start from the head and follow the silhouette, both front and back, you will be drawing several S shapes from head to bosom to back of waist to belly to hips and bottom, and, when kneeling, to thighs and calves.

There is a line I call the Curve Line which comes from the side dropping down in an S shape, outlining the edge of the belly. It is a very flowing body line.

OUTSTANDING FEATURE: Rounded, S-shape forms.

CHECK ARTWORK: *" Broadgate Venus"*- Botero.

CHECK GODDESS IMAGE: *" Armless Lady,* Balzi Rossi Caves".

Example of S-Shape Motif: " Gold Line Study Two " by T'Rina Headlee. 8" x11", gold Prismacolor pencil line drawing. © 1999 by T'Rina Headlee.

Cathy Bryant, a Tall Reubenesque, also portrays an S-shaped motif in this side view. Sports bra, bicycle shorts with white stripe down the side. Photo credit: Linda Kanzinger.

SHORTHAND DESCRIPTIONS OF PLUS AND SUPERSIZE WOMEN S SHAPES

These are short sketches, a shorthand, if you will, of the various types or shapes , both plus, and supersize.

1. Venus: she's very bosomy and has a waist.

2. Pear: she is bottom-heavy and is much smaller on top (shoulders and bust).

3. Rectangle: she doesn't have curves.

4. Renoir: the lines of her curves are very gentle and sloping.

5. Reubenesque: she is short and "stocky".

6. Apple: she has slender legs compared with her rounded upper body.

7. Scalloped: she has fat and curves and folds on the front of her body, but her backside is pretty "straight" lined.

8. Tall Reubenesque: she is tall, fat, and firm.

9. SuperPear: she is very bottom-heavy.

10. SuperVenus: she is big, she still has a waist, and a bust, and everything is pretty firm!

11. Goddess: she is big big big all put in a short package.

12. SuperReubenesque: you notice her! She has "presence". She is big and she is tall.

13. Juno: what you notice is how big and how soft she is, how multitudinous are her curves and folds.

14. Heart-Shaped: looking from behind, there are her "hearts".

15. S shaped woman: the curves of her belly and bust and behind make S shapes.

THE IMPORTANCE OF NAMING

Naming is important. By giving positive names to different body types, how we view those shapes changes. By being connected to the Goddess figures from ancient herstory, the plus and supersize shapes of women are connected to positive and powerful images. This cannot but help change the negative stereotypes of fat women! In doing the research for this book, I wanted to give special names to our large women bodies. I kept the images of all the fat women I have looked at over the years in my mind, until the right word or image came to my mind. And thus, I gave our shapes names.

WHAT IS SIZE-POSITIVE ABOUT THE LARGE WOMAN'S BODY?

SOFTNESS: large women have soft bodies. Often their bellies are soft like pillows. They have large soft breasts. Their thighs are big and soft. They are nice to touch.

WEIGHT/SUBSTANCE/HEAVINESS: Large women's bodies have substance. They are there! When you hug them, they feel substantial, solid, comforting. Hugging a large woman can bring forth a feeling of security. You can lean on her, and she won't blow away!

JIGGLE-WIGGLE: A large woman's body moves. Her fat moves. It may sway. The natural skeletal movement can swing with some "meat on the bones". Watching a large woman's body move is fascinating.

FORM: A large woman's body has form, and not all the same kind, as we have seen. There is versatility in form. It's not just a skeleton hung with skin. There is depth, there are angles to explore. It is a sculptural form to be explored visually.

6

SUCCESSFUL DESIGNS:PUTTING IT ALL TOGETHER

"Having been deprived of beautiful clothes for so long, many women have grown too comfortable using clothes as camouflage to give it up with ease. Many are just plain timid about clothes. And many, having had no use for them for so long, just do not know the principles of dressing well."

Hara Marano- *Style is Not a Size*

"THE OVER-EMPHASIS ON THE VERTICAL LINE AND THE FOCUS ON 'SLIMMING LOOKS' LIMITS DESIGN CHOICES."

Linda S. Kanzinger-*Size-Positive Style!*

A successful design works when the shape of the body and the silhouette and the general design of the clothing is harmonious. As we have seen in the chapter on The Rules, there are many fashion guidelines that restrict and constrict the phat woman's creative expression in clothing. Much of this comes from the concept of the ideal body type. I have found that most all mainstream fashion books and plus-size fashion books still embrace this concept.

But, as we have seen from the photographs of the many Rulebreakers throughout the book, there are many many successful designs and looks available to the curvaceous woman. Looking at these pictures give many ideas for how to dress in new ways. There are also certain concepts that we can explore that will help.

Capsules, colors and seasons, and **fashion principles** are three such concepts. Mainstream fashion books still have good ideas for the size-positive woman on capsule dressing, certain fashion principles, and certainly in the area of building a wardrobe. Plus-size fashion books speak to some fashion principles that are size-positive, but the book that is the most liberating in my opinion is *The Triumph of Individual Style*-Carla Mason Mathis and Helen Villa Connor.

CAPSULES

Capsules, or models, are a way of learning to put together the clothes you have in a variety of ways. It's a way of dressing that doesn't have a "cooky-cutter" stamp on it. In order to start using the concept, one has to:

• obtain a variety of clothes that fit

• be a size-positive woman who has the self-confidence to dress uniquely, and

•choose the appropriateness of the situation to the clothes.

The concept of "clothing capsules" comes from the work of Janet Wallach (*Looks that Work* and *Working Wardrobe.*) This concept uses a small number of pieces of clothing which are coordinated in color, fabric, and silhouette. The parts are all interchangeable, and you mix and match them.

She uses no more than twelve individual pieces for the capsule wardrobe. You choose a theme: either color, texture, silhouette or mood. Then you build around that theme. For example, I often wear black and purple together. I have many many clothes in both these colors, and so it is easy to throw together outfits at a moment's notice. Another theme is to emphasize texture, wearing neutral colors and emphasizing the fabrics used. Another choice is to pick a unique silhouette to make a statement.

Creative capsules push the edge a bit. It's the art of putting together colors or fabrics or accessories that normally are not worn together. Past examples include wearing plaids and stripes which would look mismatched except for the intentional look that the wearer gave it. It's fun, but it takes time. When you do pull together an unusual look, a good idea is to make notes on what clothing items and accessories you used. Next time you want that look, you won't have to start from scratch!

COLORS AND SEASONS

The concept of colors and seasons is well-known by now, and there are good books for detailed information (*Color with Style*- Donna Fujii, as well as *Always in Style with Color Me Beautiful*- Carol Jackson) on your colors and seasons. I used to feel this information was pretty "fluffy", but after doing research on it, I think it has value.

What I have learned from this concept is that certain colors do add a" lift" to your face and overall look. You want the colors you wear to lift you up in your face. Also the "right" colors will clarify your face. Some colors help to define both your face and your presence. With other colors, you will look muddied, or kind of droop into the background. No size-positive fat woman needs that!

While I don't think it is necessary to go the whole route with color matching systems, and color consultants, etc. I do think this is good knowledge to have. If you try on an outfit and you start to fade or look "muddy", then you can assess that it could be the wrong shade of color on you.

I know from personal experience the truth of this. I was told as a child that brown was a "good color" for me since my hair and eyes are brown. I wore brown for years, never even realizing how old and dowdy it made me feel. Finally I "woke up", and started to wear clothes that made me feel good inside. Brown was rarely my choice. I finally tossed most all of the brown clothes in my wardrobe, and I have never regretted it!

When buying fabric to sew clothes, simply drape the fabric across your neck and look in a mirror. Experiment with different shades of a color family to find the ones that work for you. Do the same while shopping for ready-made clothing.

As well, notice when an outfit "brings you down" either emotionally, or when you look in the mirror. Look in your wardrobe to see what colors and shades your favorite outfits are. Experiment with new shades that you haven't tried. See if they lift you up.

"She uses no more than twelve individual pieces for the capsule wardrobe.

You choose a theme: either color, texture, silhouette or mood.

Then you build around that theme."

GENERAL FASHION PRINCIPLES

> **" I refuse to accept that 2% of the female population represents the "ideal figure", and the 98% of us that are left are seen as deviant, with low-status and a socially unsanctioned body shape and size."**
> Linda S. Kanzinger, *Size-Positive Style!*
>
> "All of the so-called rules of 'fat dressing' are based on the premise that we should be trying to make ourselves look slimmer."
> Nancy Roberts, *Breaking All the Rules*

Fashion principles is the next concept that can help with successful dressing. Fashion principles are different from the rules, discussed earlier. Fashion principles can help a person understand why a certain outfit "works" or a certain look makes a phat woman more attractive than a similarly put together outfit that, for some reason, is "off". These principles can help the thick woman understand why, when she is trying on one skirt in a store, **why** it looks unattractive on her, and why another similarly styled skirt makes her look great!

In most fashion books, you will hear the words **proportion, balance, harmony,** and **emphasis** or **focal point** being discussed in terms of successful fashion designs. You will also hear the term **"the ideal figure"** and balance and proportion are discussed especially in relation to that. In *Dress Like A Million,* Leah Feldman describes the relationship between your figure plus the four major design components of a garment or outfit as creating fashion success. The four components are: **proportion, line, color and texture.** Each of these elements should be in complete harmony with each other, and with you.

The focus for most fashion writers is to **balance** the figure so it will be proportioned, and then to focus on **the vertical line** to attempt to make the figure look slimmer, or more elongated. A complex set of equations occurs, adding and subtracting here and there along the figure in order to attempt to reach this illusive "ideal figure". This is what much of the logic of the Rules is also based upon.

A thorough study of design principles would include **balance, proportion, line, color, texture, illusion, gradation, scale, rhythm, concentricity, unity, harmony, alternation, sequence, repetition, emphasis, contrast, radiation, transition, and gradation.** This is information important to fashion designers, for it makes the difference between a successful design, and an average design that doesn't sell to a wide audience. We will just touch on the basics of fashion principles in this chapter.

LINGERIE

(left) Ivory colored robe, tap pants, and camisole set worn by Kelly Ryan. She is not trying to "balance" her thick ankles or voluptuous thighs but rather to emphasize their loveliness in this romantic, graceful outfit. Photo credit: Photos by Beth, Mpls, MN.

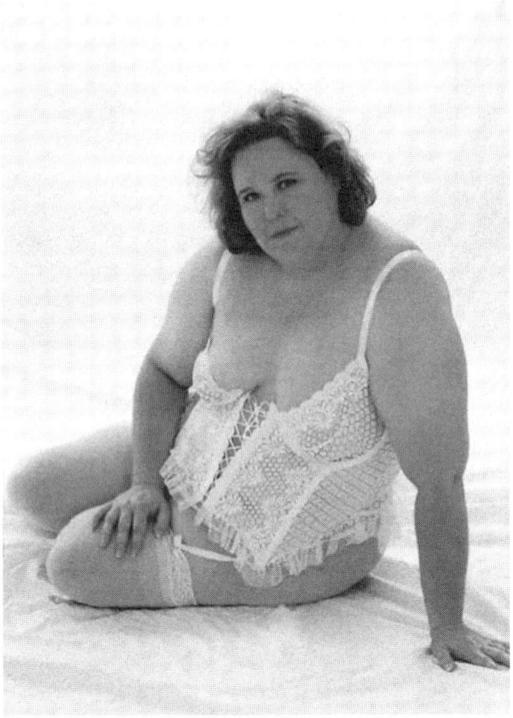

(above) Romantic looking ivory colored Victorian lace teddy lingerie with garters and matching hosiery. Photo credit: Voluptuous Images.

(above right) Kelly Ryan portrays another view of the ivory tap pants, camisole, and robe set. Camisole, tap pants, size LT, nylon/polyester blend; robe 100% polyester, size 2X. Photo Credit: Photos by Beth, Mpls, MN. (right) Kelly Ryan in a red and black teddy made from satin-nylon lace, size 40. Photo credit: Jim Woosley@ Jim Woosley Photograph, Mpls, MN

(above left) Bella models purple teddy in satin and lace. Photo credit: John B. King.
(above right) Stacey Richardson wears a black leather teddy with studs, with net robe. Both size 26/28W. From Barb's Large and Lovely.
(below left) Enid Caccavelli wears a black lace lingerie outfit, size L, 100% nylon. Photo credit: Tom Caccavelli.
(below right) Pink baby doll lingerie with sheer skirt and panties, and ribbon ruffled bra top. Photo credit: Voluptuous Images.

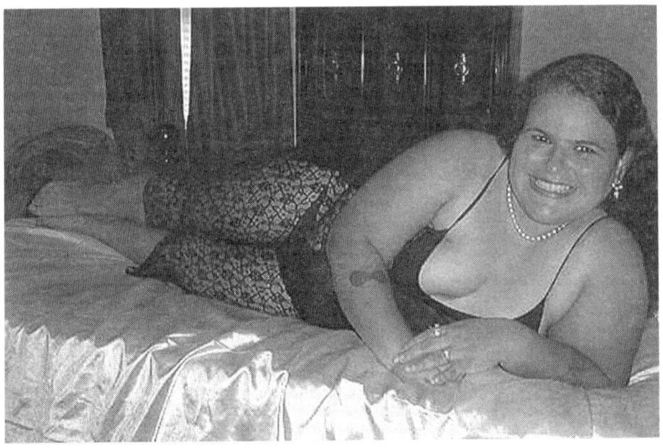

(above left) Cleacia Foster models baby blue bra, size 44DD, nylon/lycra blend, with white feather boa. Photo credit: Skip Orlando. (below) Cathy Bryant wearing a peach colored print slipdress, 100% polyester. Photo credit: Linda Kanzinger.

THE IDEAL FIGURE

The conventional wisdom about the ideal figure is to draw it in a ratio of head lengths: 8:1. This came from the artist Leonardo da Vinci's image of the ideal figure. It is based on an ideal figure with an illusion of symmetrical features. Now, less than 2% of women fit the "ideal woman" and, as we all know, that ideal type shifts. In *Dress Like A Million*, Leah Feldon says the proportional idea changes, and today leans towards tall and lanky, as epitomized by the world's top supermodels. This is why, for fashion models, the figure is **elongated** to 8 1/2 head lengths. This is an ever so slightly changing "ideal female form" proposed and promoted by a size discriminist and sexist society. It is out of touch with reality, and real women.

The ideal figure is sometimes called a symmetrical figure. The goal of symmetry wants everyone's body to look as close to this illusionary "ideal" as possible, so everyone's body is camouflaged to attempt to fit this standard. The focus is to create an ideal figure with each and every style. Fashion writers, both mainstream and plus-size, discuss the fashion principles of **balance, harmony, the vertical line,** and **proportion** with the goal of making the fat body appear like the ideal. But, does it work, or does it simply block a woman from dressing creatively and with flair?

Traditional fashion views the ideal body shape as the key to all design decisions. After that, they are influenced by the fashions of proportional

ideals. Presently, a long slender look is preferred. It is assumed that everyone wants to "try" and look this way. This has not always been the case. The tightly laced corset to show a wasp waist, or the bustle to presume a well-endowed rear end, or the crinolines of other historical times were the results of a different proportional ideal.

Proportional ideals change through time.

One could ask: how "ideal" are they?

ALTERNATIVE VIEWS

It is an interesting mental exercise if a person throws out the idea of the "ideal" figure type. What happens then? The first image that comes to my mind is that of each individual person with unique characteristics, which would not, uncommonly, fall into various groups. Women with large shoulders; women with large breasts; women with big bones and long legs, etc. I would add to this that we can also de-emphasize the less interesting or less attractive parts of our bodies.

But we, as individuals, would make this definition. I feel that the healthy woman can use both of these to her advantage. She can emphasize her natural assets; and she can de-emphasize, by using the tools and techniques of illusion, the areas of the body **she** chooses to de-emphasize.

A few other fashion writers also have had

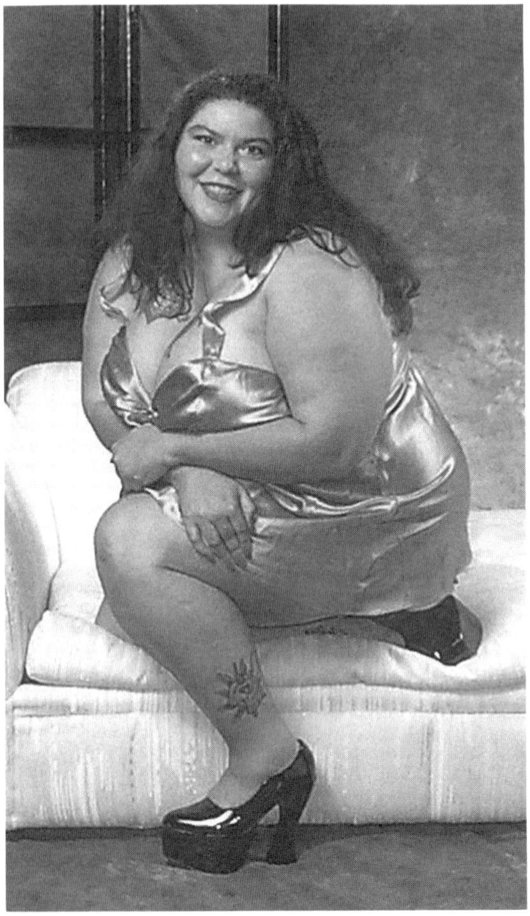

(above) Cleacia Foster wearing a shiny silvery slipdress, polyester, size 26/28W, with equally shiny black platform shoes. Photo credit: Skip Orlando. (below) Cathy Bryant models a wine-colored velveteen slipdress, 100% polyester. Photo credit: Linda Kanzinger.

(above) Cleacia Foster wearing a red satin bra, size 46DD, and panties, size 26/28W, with maroon velvet coat and black heels. Photo credit: Skip Orlando.

differing views. David Kibbe's book *Metamorphosis* is one. Kibbe refuted this idea of the ideal figure in 1988, which was at its time, very progressive. Instead of "evening out your features", he talks about each person having a "central essence" and "discovering your theme". He stressed **balance** as opposed to **symmetry.** The concept of balance stresses enhancing your natural features. He said we should throw out the idea of the ideal figure, and instead, emphasize the interesting and unique parts of our figures. The goal is to wear clothes which accentuate unique features and look for the positive in a unique feature, rather than trying to downplay it.

"To dress in accordance with this new philosophy, one would just 'follow one's body'."

For example, a woman with large hips, rather than wearing shoulder pads or a boxy blazer in an attempt to try to "balance" her figure would see this as a unique feature and could include wearing clothes which instead **featured** her large hips! It's simply a matter of "reframing" how we look at various body shapes. A large-bosomed woman would celebrate this feature—not hide it— and when the mood arose, wear tight sweaters.

Another book which offers an alternative view of fashion principles is *The Triumph of Individual Style,* by Carla Mason Mathis and Helen Villa Connor. They use countless images from art to illustrate various body shapes, and show ways to emphasize or de-emphasize different parts of the anatomy without putting judgments on these different parts. This lack of judgment is truly refreshing! I'm not quite sure what it is that makes certain shapes more or less attractive than others, or if it is truly only cultural. But, with an artists' eye, everything can be looked at differently, and ultimately, with a size-positive view.

Using art principles as fashion principles allows for much creativity. There is choice. There is not an imposed body standard, as there is with the ideal figure type. There is personal choice to **highlight, camouflage, balance,** and otherwise portray various parts of the figure as well as the entire figure. Figure "parts" (called Body Particulars by Mathis and Connor) here include the following: face, neck, shoulders, back, chest, bosom, rib cage, waist, arms and hands, stomach, rear end, thighs, legs and feet.

Fashion principles based on art principles are freeing in a way that fashion principles based on the traditional ways of thinking about the ideal figure are not.

> **"There is no judgment of what is 'good' or 'bad' as is so often seen in most mainstream and plus-size fashion books.**
>
> **There are no 'figure flaws' or 'figure challenges'."**

FASHION PRINCIPLES AND VALUE JUDGMENTS IN PLUS-SIZE FASHION BOOKS

Plus-size (I know of no exclusively supersize fashion book writers at this time) fashion book writers are of two minds when discussing fashion principles. Some have an experimental attitude of "just try it"! The suggestions are not based on a philosophy of camouflaging a " bad" body, but rather of design and fashion principles .

However, other plus-size fashion writers also use terminology like "problem area", "challenge areas", and suggest we " highlight attributes", or "detract from our flaws", or "conceal all our flaws". Or they imply that our big arms are "a sensitive issue". All of these terms place **value judgments** on the shapes of our various body parts.

Now, in truth, fashion principles shouldn't have values. They are abstract concepts, but they are used to place value judgments upon body shapes. Let's try and break this down. For example:

- **To highlight is a fashion principle**
- **It has no value judgment**

(below) Cleacia Foster wearing black net catsuit, size 28W. Photo credit: Skip Orlando.

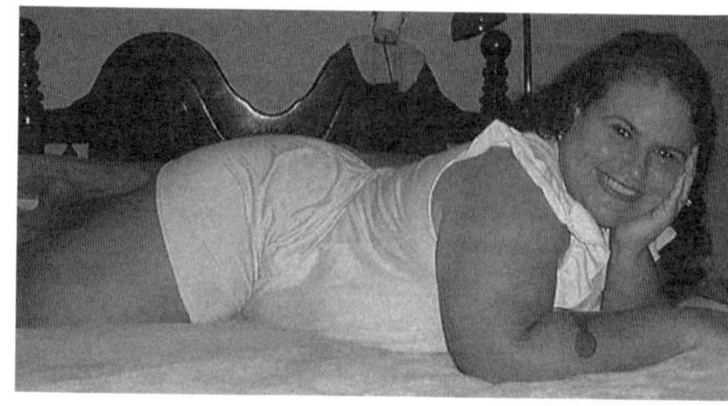

(above right) Enid Caccavelli wearing 100% baby blue polyester Victorian pajamas with white lace trim, size L. Photo credit: Tom Caccavelli.

(above left) Ivory Victorian style slip, 100% cotton. Photo credit: Voluptuous Images.

(above)Who says voluptuous women can't find sexy lingerie! Cleacia Foster models black lace bra, size 46DD, with panties, 26/28W, along with a shiny purple shirt, size 22/24W. All nylon/lycra blend. Photo credit: Skip Orlando.

CATSUITS

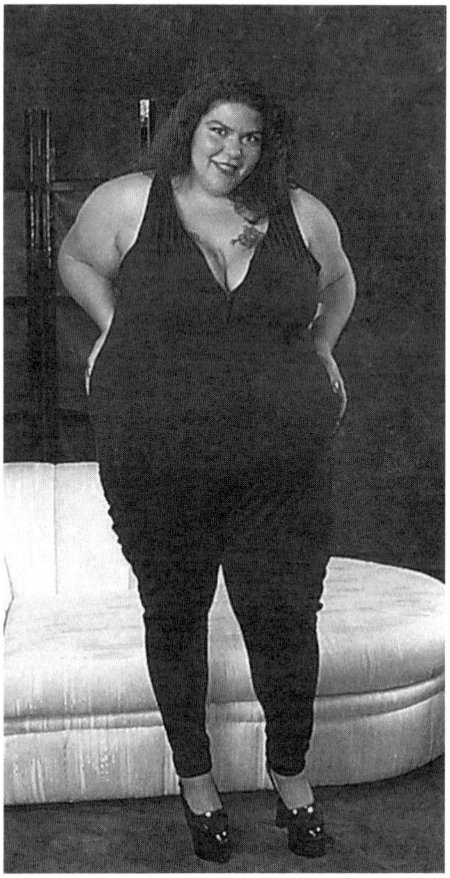

(above left) Stacey Richardson models a black catsuit of a spandex/nylon blend from Barb's Large and Lovely, size 26/28W

(below left) Gabrielle Sparapani is hanging out in the bedroom talking on the phone while she relaxes in her jammies, a 100% polyester nightshirt, size 24W.

(below right) 100% cotton floral pajamas. Photo credit: Voluptuous Images.

(above) Cleacia Foster wears a black catsuit and shiny black platform shoes. Catsuit, size 5X, from Love Your Peaches. Cotton interlock fabric. Photo credit: Skip Orlando.

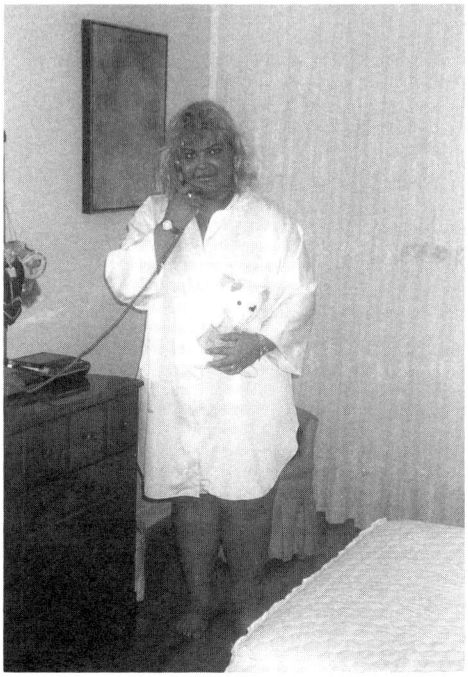

SLEEPWEAR

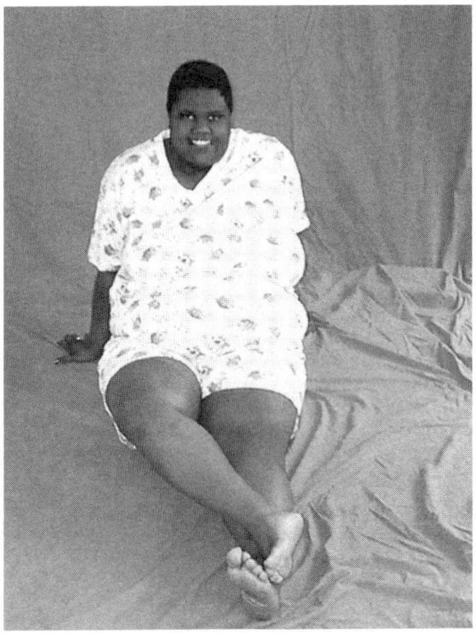

WEDDING DRESSES

(above) A lovely white satin and lace wedding gown with net train and upper bodice. Gabrielle Sparapani is the bride.

Isn't this a surprise! A pleased and happy Teresa Marie Metcalfe-Johnson with her husband, Lonnie Johnson, in her bridal dress, size 26W, an Alfred Angelo design, heavy white satin with lace bodice and sleeves embellished with pearls. Photo credit: Jessie Rouse.

(left) A view of Gabrielle Sparapani's wedding dress showing the long train. (right) Linda Kanzinger on her special day wearing her silk wedding dress which she designed and sewed herself, size 22W. Pongee silk, silk chiffon, and lace.

(lower left) Sharon Klose in her wedding dress, with her husband John. White satin with pearl beads and shimmer sequin accents. Lace overlay on bodice. Size 28 1/2W. Photo credit: Perri Neri. (lower right) Ronda Gregoire in her wedding dress with train and floral arrangement, size 22W. Photo credit: Cindy Butterfield @ Dynamic Photography.

(above) Teresa Marie Metcalfe-Johnson's gown with train. Heavy white satin, lace bodice. Size 26W. Photo credit: Jessie Rouse.

(above) Stella Kuperberg in her lovely bridal dress with long train. Satin, cotton, lace for the neck area, sequins, artificial pearls, and rhinestones. With all these gems, the dress ended up weighing 21 pounds! (right) Another elegant bridal design, by Paula Sanders Couture, Mpls,MN. Kelly Ryan in her wedding dress, size 20, ivory and pink dull satin, with rose bouquet. Photo credit: Trotter Photo, St. Louis, MO.

- **Unstated is the" value judgment" of body parts**

- **Slim legs are "good" while a rounded apple shaped upper body is " bad"**

The writer then jumps over the unstated value judgments and then make a fashion pronouncement: wear the wedged-shaped sheath or a big shirt over leggings, designs which **emphasize** the slim legs of the Apple shape. They always wax euphoric over "her slim legs", and all the things she can wear to highlight her slim legs. Suggestions are made to wear shoulder pads to **balance** the large hips and thighs of the Pear, and Venus is of course told to wear straight-line designs, and perhaps a minimizer bra, to **"minimize"** what are simply her womanly curves.

With these **body parts values** firmly in place, these writers go ahead and describe a series of principles to which, if one works it out, will make your figure as close to the principles of the "ideal figure" as possible. They never suggest :

- **revealing or highlighting big hips, thighs, or the derriere of the Pear shape.**

- **revealing the apple shape of the Apple, instead they only focus on the slender legs.**

DRESSES

A Venus or X shape is never encouraged to:

- **highlight her small waist or large breasts**
- **wear tight knit sweaters or tops**
- **wear waist-cinching belts to outline a waistline**

People who view our various body parts with these value judgments are generally aiming at using the fashion principles of **balance** and **proportion** with the goal of making our body appear as close as possible to the "ideal figure".

Rather than splitting the body off into good parts/bad parts, and focus on trying to make each unique body shape as close as can be to the current Ideal (the 2% of the female population, by the way)

> **"my size-positive view is to see the body shapes as a part of the whole and not assign them value."**
>
> "Then you can **choose** what you want to **focus on, highlight, emphasize** in one outfit and **choose a totally different emphasis in another."**

DRESSY DRESSES

(above) Teresa Maria Metcalfe-Johnson in a black lacy dress, size 26W. Photo credit: Satu. (left) Cleacia Foster in a long sleeved black full-length formal dress, size 4X, from Love Your Peaches. Velvet and georgette. Photo credit: Skip Orlando.

(right) Stacey Richardson in an elegant formal long white silk brocade dress, size 26/28W. Thigh-high slit, with seed pearls and sequins. (far right) Emanon models a raw silk dress, size 24W, sand colored, with dark brown rayon scarf. Photo credit: Vic Toliva.

(below) Stacey Richardson models an elegant black two piece evening dress, (sleeveless dress with matching jacket) in a spandex/nylon lycra blend fabric, size 26/28W. A Vikki Vi design with a silver silk embroidered medallion front.

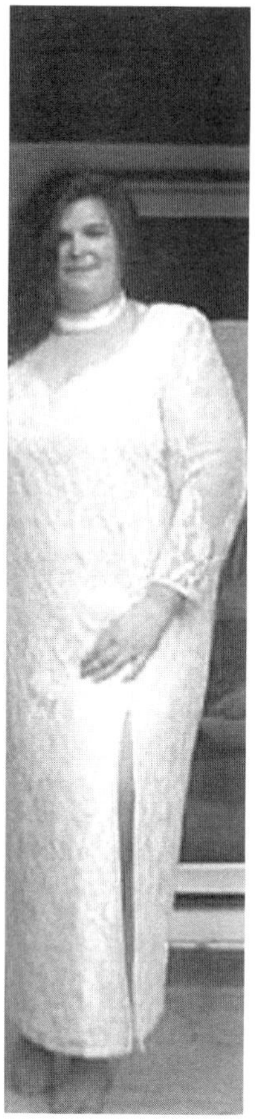

(below) Sharon Klose relaxes in a formal cream-colored gown. Size 6 from Love Your Peaches. 100% silk full skirt; bodice 20% spandex, 60% cotton, 20% nylon. Photo credit: Perri Neri.

(Above) Cat Nordling wears a black print We Be Bop crinkle rayon dress with beaded front bodice. Hats are printed in the black background of the bodice/sleeves/patch pockets/skirt hem. The main skirt piece is a black and white blotch print. From Dayton's, 2X. With strap purse. (Right upper and lower)) Cat is wearing a sleeveless smoke-blue empire style "Crystal dress" with flowing chiffon panels over silk satin with hanging Venice lace at hem. The top is a collage of Venice lace for support. From La Reina Boutique, Inc. Size 4X. Photo credit for all three: Staci Gilbert.

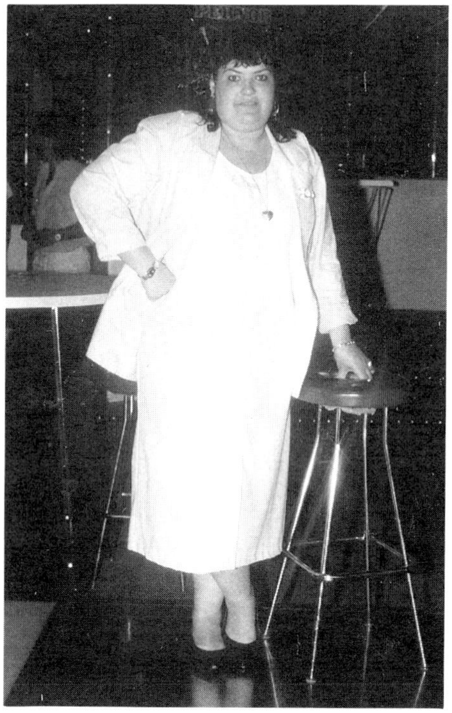

COTTON DRESSES

"NOW, WHAT HAPPENS IF
WE REMOVE THAT CONCEPT FROM
OUR THINKING,
AND LOOK AT THE
PRINCIPLES OF THE FOCAL
POINT OR HIGHLIGHTING,
CAMOUFLAGE,
PROPORTION,
BALANCE,
LINE,
COLOR,
TEXTURE, AND
SILHOUETTE,
FREE OF THE NEED TO
APPROXIMATE **THE**
IDEAL FIGURE.
WHAT WILL HAPPEN
THEN?"

(above left) Gabrielle Sparapani wearing a stonewashed bluejean outfit, a denim skirt and blouse. (lower left) Gabrielle Sparapani models a casual button-down-the-front bluejean dress with fluted hem. Notice how the eye travels down the line of buttons to the design detail of the fluted hem for an elegant flowing line.

FASHION PRINCIPLES BASED ON ART: HIGHLIGHT AND CAMOUFLAGE

Let's first go back to the book that I mentioned before, *The Triumph of Individual Style* by Carla Mason Mathis and Helen Villa Connor, and look at their fashion principles based on art. Nowhere in these principles is there mention of having to balance a figure part in order to try to approximate an "ideal figure".

Their philosophy is one of choice— and they offer two basic ways for us to approach our figure. One way is to **highlight** a specific part; the other way is to **camouflage** it. At no time do they make any value judgments on our body shapes and parts.

For example, they present thick or heavy ankles, and then give suggestions for **both** highlighting and camouflaging! This shows the radical concept of this book: that both are acceptable.

I welcome the concepts in *The Triumph of Individual Style,* because this is, to my knowledge, the first book that challenges the dominance of the "ideal figure" while not throwing fashion out the window. In fact, it is a highly researched book taking into consideration a wide range of fashion options and body styles.

"I personally believe that fashion principles based on art are free of the sexist attitudes implicit in the 'ideal body type'."

TANK DRESSES

(above right) Myra Turley models a cotton knit black tank dress, from Magical Creations, of Portland, OR, size 4, with a green cotton crinkle cloth jacket, size 4, with a medallion necklace. Photo credit: Linda Kanzinger. (right) Cathy Bryant wears a mustard colored tank dress with yellow sandals and long red scarf. Dress, 100% polycotton. Photo credit: Linda Kanzinger.

SUITS

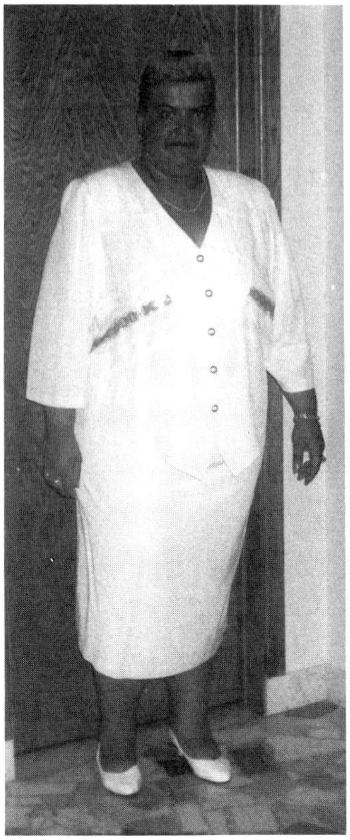

(above) Kelly Ryan modeling a forest green suit from Venezia, a linen/rayon blend with poly lining, size 22, wiht white hose and matching green pumps. Photo credit: David P Bouckaert, St. Louis, MO. (Above right) Gabrielle Sparapani models a Michael Antoni white suit with gold stripes on the side. Size 22/24W. (right) Andrea Hall in a navy blue suit with a white collar, and white hose, size 24W. Photo credit: Linda Kanzinger.

DRESSY SEPARATES/CLUB CLOTHES

(above left) Sherry Lynette models a dressy separates outfit of sheer nylon white blouse with U-neck, button front, faux pearl buttons, size 18/20 with black floor length pleated slacks , nylon/rayon blend size 16/18. Vintage cameo necklace. Photo credit: © Monico Candelaria/Photographer.

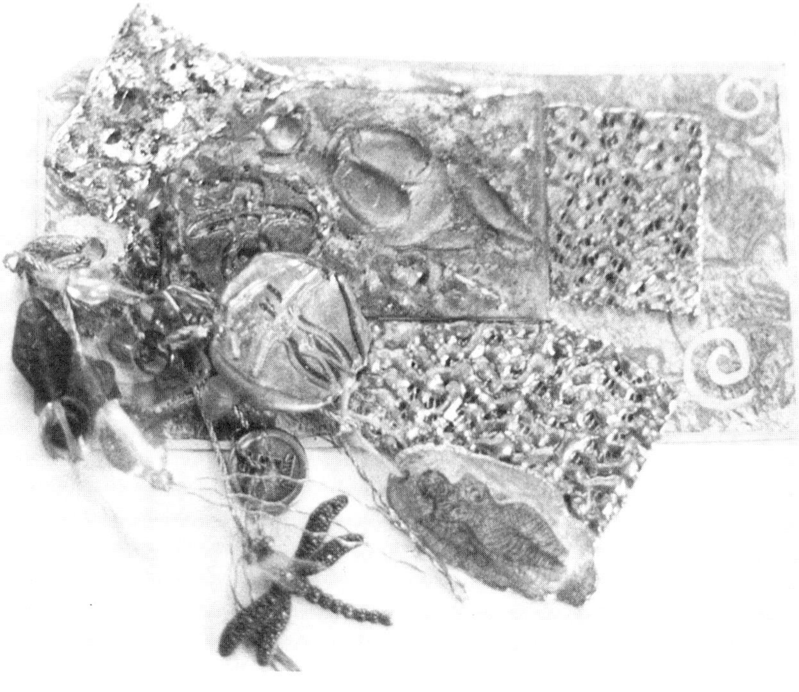

Tag, rubber stamped with images of goddess women, stamps from Her Rubber. Thick embossing powders, glitters, trinkets, ribbons, and embellishments by Kim Caldwell. Photo credit: Linda Kanzinger.

(above right) Cleacia Foster relaxing in a black lace halter, 1X, from Barb's Large and Lovely; faux leather black pants from Bodacious Babes in Boston, size 3X and silver cotton/poly blend jacket, size 4X from La Reina Boutique, Inc. Photo credit: Skip Orlando.

(upper left) Emanon in a black velvet spaghetti strap top, size XL, with a black velvet skirt, size 2X; also with long-sleeved cotton and lace blouse, size XL. Photo credit Vic Toliva, Detroit, MI. (upper right) Gabrielle Sparapani in a black and white vest, with rayon white shirt. (lower right) Delores Young is wearing a brightly patterned blazer of a brocade fabric, with long slacks and a matching turtleneck pullover. The curved lines in the elegant brocade blazer harmonize with her curvy figure! Photo credit: Kim Caldwell.

SIZE-POSITIVE FASHION PRINCIPLES: PROPORTION AND BALANCE

Another fashion principle besides balancing the figure that is important to our discussion is proportion. I've read the word proportion countless times but didn't really understand it until I read the book *Dress Like a Million* by Leah Feldon. In her chapter, "Go Figure" she very succinctly explains the concept of proportion. She describes it as "interdependent space-size relationships". It's a **relationship** between shapes and sizes, and so you can play with it. You can, therefore, either "complement" your body shape or you can "balance it".

Proportion is the relationship between different size or shapes of the body. If one part looks bigger, proportion means the other part automatically looks smaller. If you appear shorter wearing something, it must appear longer. Like two ends of a teeter-totter:

- **long________short**
- **wider_______narrower**
- **bigger______smaller**

The fashion ideal, ie "well dressed" or a simple "that looks good on you" is when the proportions of your body and your clothes are in harmony. The combination of all these **shapes** creates the physical make-up of each individual.

- **the size of our head,**
- **the distance from our head to our waist**
- **the length of our torso**
- **the length of our legs**

Other body shapes reveal horizontal lines. These include:

- **our shoulders**
- **the bustline**
- **the waist**

Fashion principles can be abstract, hard to grasp at first. Experimenting with outfits is one good way to figure out what looks good on you. When you find an outfit that "works", write it down, and then try to study why it works. Use your own fashion principles to guide you as you expand your style!

(above right) F. Tara Weber shows how well a long tube skirt works on a curvy figure. Pink knit V-neck top, black stretch long skirt, and chunky sandals. Size 14/16W. Photo credit: Michael Gomez.

(lower right) Tesia Johnson pauses in a pensive mood in a doorway, wearing a brown button-down jacket, 100% polyester, size 28W, with flower print skirt, 100% polyester, size 26W. Photo credit: Hansi, Oakland, CA.

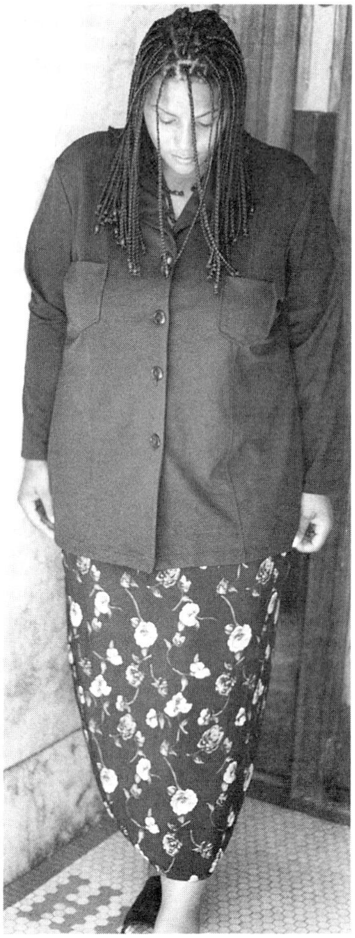

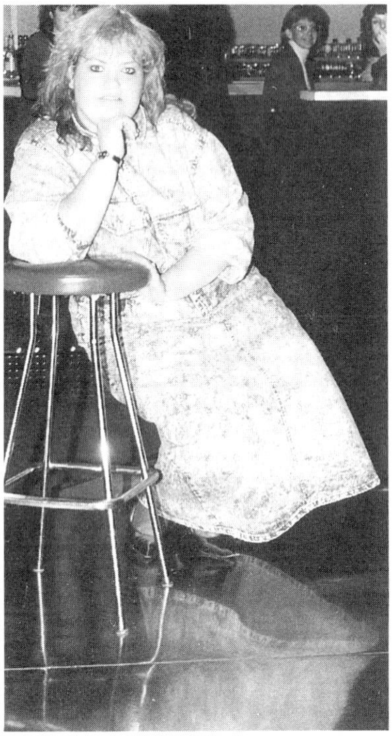

CASUAL SEPARATES:
BLOUSES, TOPS, SKIRTS, PANTS, VESTS, JACKETS, SWEATERS, BLUEJEANS

(upper left) Gabrielle Sparapani in her favorite two-piece stone wash jean outfit, size 22W. (upper right) Tesia Johnson wears a brown button-down suede jacket, size 26/28W with brown slacks, 100% polyester, size 28W. Photo credit: Hansi, Oakland, CA. (lower right) Gabrielle Sparapani is relaxing in a casual outfit of a turtleneck sweater, black jeans and black suspenders.

(upper right) Relaxing on the bed, Stella Kuperberg sports close-fitting jeans and a casual top. Photo credit: Kevin Kuperberg. (center left) Gabby Sparapani relaxing in bluejeans and a blue sleeveless pullover top.

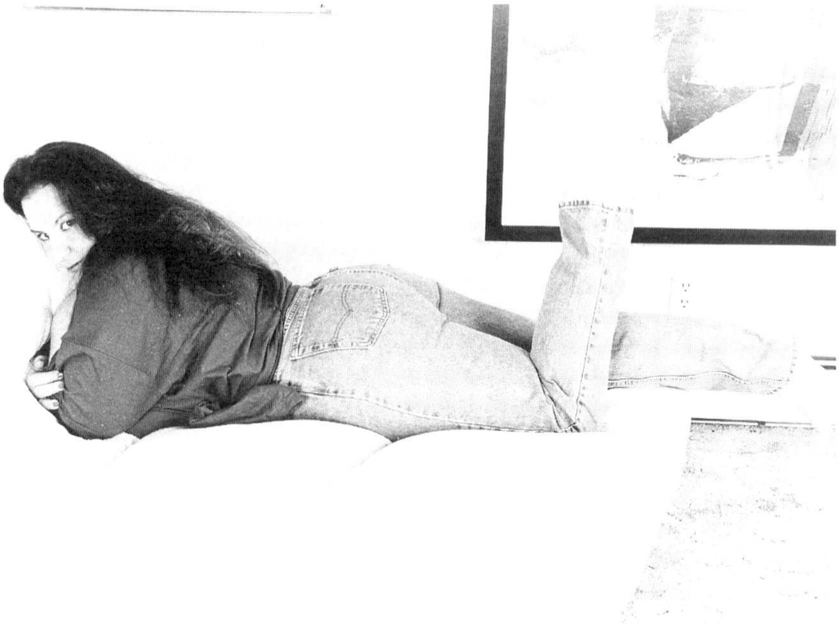

(center right) F. Tara Weber is wearing stone-washed blue jeans and a red sweater. 14/16. (lower right) Jennie Middleton in a white cotton tank top 2X, blue sweatshirt, 3X, blue jeans size 28W with blue-striped white Adidas and to top it off, pink sunglasses!

SHORTS AND TOPS

Enid Caccavelli washing the car in her beige shorts, 20W, poly/cotton blend, with black string top size 39, 100% nylon. Photo credit: Tom Caccavelli.

Linda Kanzinger carries her niece, Robin Kanzinger, up the Timberline trail, Mt Hood, Oregon, approximately 12,000 feet in elevation. White rayon top, 20W, cotton gabardine running shorts with bias tape edging, designed by the author by grading a pattern made from a pair of men's XL running shorts up to size 22W, slip-on cotton shoes. Photo credit: Bob Kanzinger.

Kim Caldwell in front of Okanagan Lake, Kelowna Canada, wearing a pair of red cotton shorts, 18W, and tank top, XL. Photo credit: Harris McRae.

SIZE-POSITIVE FASHION PRINCIPLES: LINE

Line is another important fashion principle. Line can be **vertical, horizontal, diagonal, or curved.** Line is found both in **the silhouette** and in the **clothing details** , or **design lines**, as well as in **the body.**

- **Body lines** are components such as **seams, darts, and tucks,** which reinforce the lines of the body

- **Silhouette lines** are the basic shape of the garment

- **Detail lines** are lines within the silhouette. They are **horizontal, vertical, diagonal, straight, or diagonally curved lines**

A line will be dominant if it is **wider, brighter, longer, or repeated more often.** Using one of these elements is a good way to plan a design.

THE OVEREMPHASIS ON THE VERTICAL LINE

Unfortunately, lines are also given value judgments. Horizontal, or **"fat" lines,** are implied to be "bad", while vertical lines (the **"thin" lines**) are "good".

In most mainstream and plus size fashion books, the vertical line is highly overemphasized. Monochromatic colors create one unbroken vertical line which makes a person appear taller. Monochromatic colors are also encouraged because there is no "line break" which would create a horizontal line.

When you are fat, you already have a lot of horizontal body line, so, according to this philosophy, you will want to " balance" it with a heavy use of the vertical line. This will nudge you towards the "ideal". If you are a fat woman wearing a miniskirt and a long-lined blazer jacket, all in a pale yellow with an even paler yellow silk blouse, there is no line break created by the colors of the clothes.

Thus, the vertical line stands!

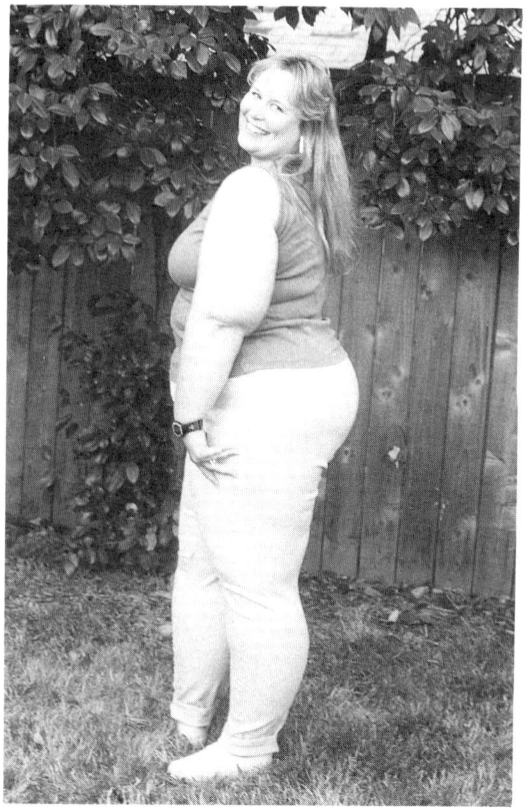

(above) Cathy Bryant in a pair of light tan stretch jeans with an olive green tank top. Photo credit: Linda Kanzinger. (below) Myra Turley in an enthusiastic moment, wearing a 100% cotton T-shirt, size 8X, and cotton denim jeans, size 4, from Making It Big. Photo credit: Linda Kanzinger.

Will you look **"less fat, ie less horizontal"** by the strength of this vertical line? I don't think so! As well, the over-emphasis on the vertical line and the focus on "slimming looks" limits design choices.

> **"What is being implied is that the horizontal line— the 'fat line'— is bad, and you shouldn't wear it, but focus instead on the vertical line. Size-positive fashion says you can wear both! When we quit focusing on having to look thin, ie emphasizing and obsessing all clothing design around vertical lines, we can focus instead on looking good!"**

THE IMPORTANCE OF THE HORIZONTAL LINE

The horizontal line is also important. It's fun to wear striped fabric, such as in striped long-sleeved cotton shirts. Stripes are used in all sorts of ways, what with horizontal stripes used on the borders of culottes or clamdiggers, as well as in skirts. Vertical and horizontal stripes can be used together in one outfit in lots of fun and imaginative ways. We as phat women don't want to feel marginalized; we also want to have fun wearing horizontal striped tops along with a vertical stripe print pants and a matching jacket!

THE DIAGONAL LINE

The diagonal line is flattering to the abundant woman. Diagonal lines are created in a number of ways. Sometimes two different colors of fabric are used in a dress with the fabrics being sewn together on the diagonal. Or, a short bodice made from two triangular shapes meet at the center of the bodice, creating diagonal lines. Diagonal lines create visual interest. As they wrap around the curves of the bodacious phat woman they create even more visual interest. (See top left photo on page 137 for an example of this). Diagonal lines also contribute to where the focal point is on a particular outfit.

(Above) White shorts and a lime green sleeveless tee makes for comfortable summer living! Cathy Bryant models. Photo credit: Linda Kanzinger. (below) Horizontal stripes are very flattering when worn with a short black skirt and strappy sandels! Photo credit: Voluptuous Images.

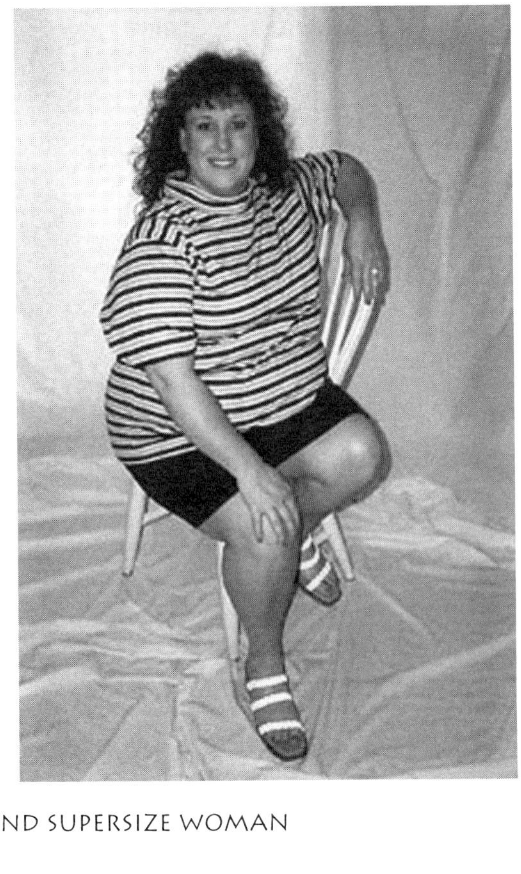

BLAZERS AND JACKETS

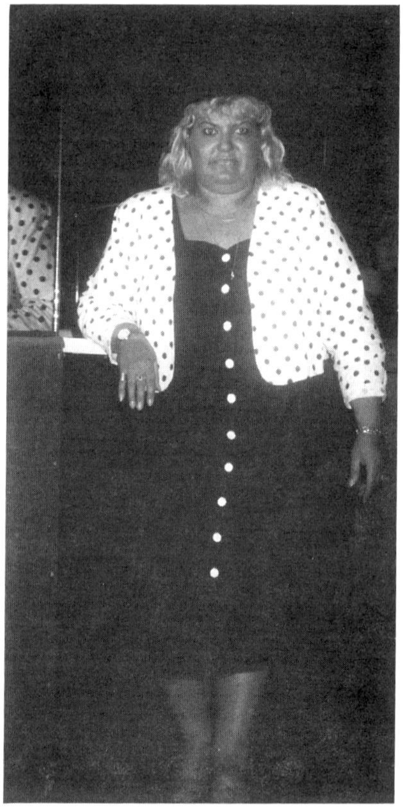

Gabby Sparapani in a 100% cotton evening dress with polka dot jacket, size 22W. See how the polka dots repeat the dotted "line" made by the white buttons on a dark fabric. (below) Gabby in dark colored dress with print jacket over it. Cotton acetate blend, size 22/24W.

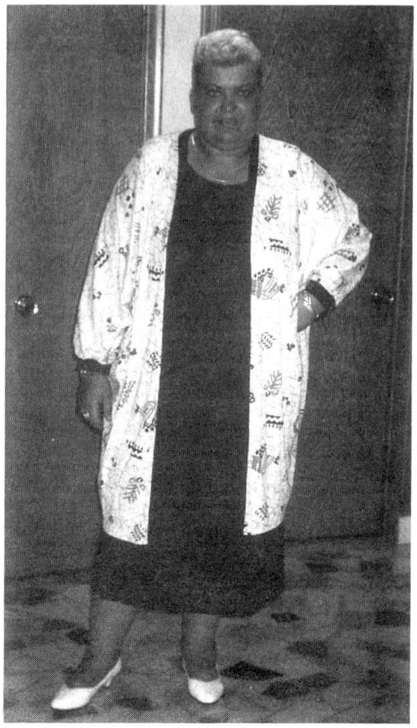

This is an example of the " long over long" silhouette. Also, because the dress is dark and the jacket is light-colored, the eye follows the jacket line down to the matching light-colored shoes.

THE CURVED LINE

The curved line is probably the most important one for us full-figured women to consider, with our rounded bodies. The curved line fits our bodies shapes, so it is the most harmonious with our shapes. Look for curved lines in clothing, such as in skirts with tapered hems (the curve follows the hips and tapers down to the edge of the skirt); knit fabrics, which naturally follow the delicious curves of our womanly bodies; and in pleated or gathered waistlines on pants or skirts, which create a curve line to follow over the belly.

CONTRADICTORY LINES AND PARALLEL LINES

I tried on a shirt with a back yoke that was wide and curved downward. It didn't look good on me, but I didn't know why. I did notice, however, that the line was contradictory to the lines of my shoulders, which are wide and straight across.

I continued to try on shirts, all the while noticing the design lines of the yoke. I realized that the shirts which looked good on my broad shoulders included shirts with tails, and with straight-line yokes which paralleled or duplicated the lines of my back.

CHOOSE YOUR LINES

As you look at yourself more and more, you will notice when you like an outfit where the various parts of the garment "hit" you at different places on your body. You can observe these fashion or design lines and be intentional in creating outfits that utilize these lines.

SIZE-POSITIVE FASHION PRINCIPLES: TEXTURE

Texture of fabric can enhance the jiggle and wiggle of the curvaceous size-positive body. Notice texture in your outfits. Put outfits together so that one texture predominates. If you are wearing a nubby sweater, have the pants be smooth-textured. Texture is subtle, not something that most people notice consciously. The phat woman can wear texture such as bulky thick sweaters and corduroy or other ribbed fabrics.

The key is in being aware of the textures that

your various outfits emote. Fabrics with texture include those that are stiff and bulky as well as smooth-flowing fabrics. Shiny or sparkly fabrics, such as ones with metallic threads, add texture and weight to the fabric. In general, if the fabric is stiffer, the design of the clothing is kept simpler. Smooth-flowing fabrics such as velour or terrycloth combine texture with more drapability, so clothing can be made with more detail or complexity.

SIZE-POSITIVE FASHION PRINCIPLES: COLOR

Use color to highlight a certain part of your shape. Light colors bring attention to the shape or part of the body, while dark colors draw attention away, or seek to minimize attention. A Superpear could wear a peach-colored skirt to draw attention to her generous hips and thighs. Pay no attention to these silly rules about minimizing and slenderizing. We have choices!

SIZE-POSITIVE FASHION PRINCIPLES: THE FOCAL POINT

The focal point of an outfit is the point at which the eye is first drawn. There are wonderful clothing designs using V-shapes or diagonals, either created by seams, decorative piping or buttons, or from the fabric print itself, which are stunning on the voluptuous figure.

You can choose where you want to put the focus, the attention. It can be hips, bustline, elbows—whatever! That's part of the fun of dressing the abundant figure—there's a big canvas and we have many places to focus our attention!

Linda Kanzinger stays warm while gazing at the Yaak River in Idaho. 100% wool sweater, in purples, blues,and greens, XXL, with 100% wool navy pants, XL. But why isn't she wearing any gloves?

PERSONAL MUSINGS

My suggestions about all these rules are : "Start from another premise. Start with seeing your large body as beautiful. Celebrate what you have. And work from there."

For example, large hips are very womanly and can be very attractive by being shown. You don't have to look cheap or gaudy either. I have large breasts and have always worn tight tops and sweaters to show them off. I also had, in my twenties and thirties, quite an hourglass figure, and I wore belts to emphasize my small waist (even though I was always a big woman).

When I was in high school, however, I remember being shamed about my womanly shape and was encouraged to wear those overblouses, tunics, long vests and rolled up sleeves in the summertime to avoid revealing my upper arm. (I weighed 135-140 lbs at the time!)

Ironically, even though "only" weighing 155-160lbs in my early twenties, I continued to unconsciously feel ashamed on a social level, though privately I always thought I had a very pretty body. It wasn't until I was around twenty seven years old, living in a more liberal environment, before I began to throw off those social feelings that I had "something to hide." (By this time I weighed around 175 lbs).

Ironically, at a heavier weight and a bigger shape, I felt more liberated!

What I didn't realize in those early years was that believing in The Rules taught me shame—it taught me to be afraid of my body and ashamed of its' womanliness.

I finally started risking—tucking my blouses in, showing my body for what it is, wearing short, waist length vests rather than long boxy ones, wearing short shorts in the summer and sleeveless tops like everybody else! I started the long journey of feeling more confident, regardless of what other people thought, and that showed in an air of self-confidence I now have (at size 20/22W weight 220 age 42 height 5'4")

Now I'm 49, and still feel just fine about my body, weigh 225 lbs and still stand 5'4"! And I never have given into the pressure of dieting!

Linda Kanzinger

SWEATERS

(upper left) Norwegians must love winter! Linda Kanzinger wearing a black wool skirt, 20W, handknit leggings, boots, and white winter sweater with border, M, 55% ramie/45% cotton. Furry pink gloves keep her hands warm, and a wine-colored mohair scarf and purple tam complete this winter outfit. Taken at Laurelhurst Park, Portland, Oregon.

(upper right) Gabby Sparapani, of Canada, models a casual rib knit sweater, size 24W. Loosely fitting thick sweaters make comfortable winter wear.

(lower right) Linda Kanzinger pauses while skiing in Wisconsin, wearing a pair of 100% Navy wool pants, XL, and a handknit sweater which she designed and made. Wool and acrylic yarn. Size 20W. Handknit tam 100% wool, also designed and made by the author.

BATHING SUITS

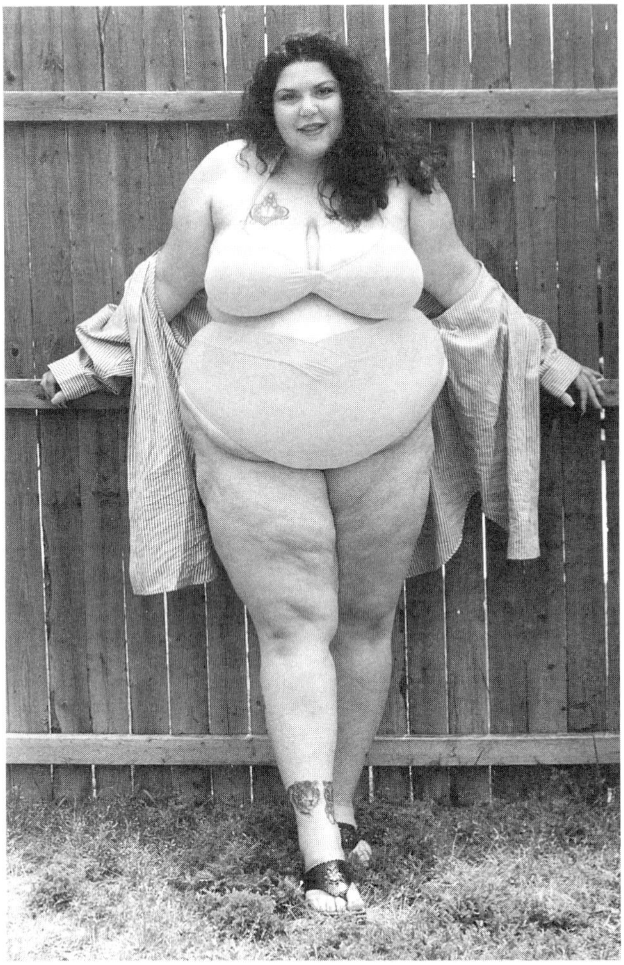

(Above left) Plenty of curves in this revealing pink bikini from Love Your Peaches. Lycra blend, top 4X, bottom, 3X. Cleacia Foster does the honors! Photo credit: Skip Orlando.

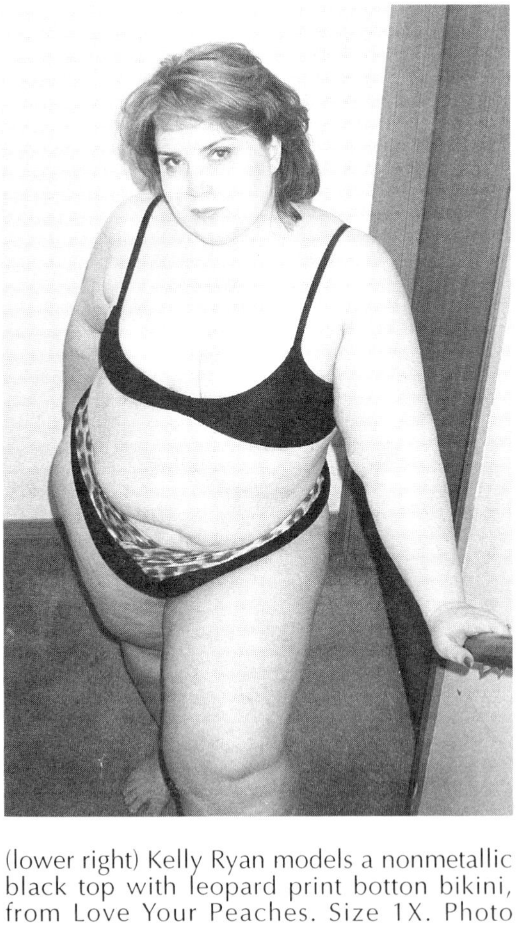

(lower right) Kelly Ryan models a nonmetallic black top with leopard print botton bikini, from Love Your Peaches. Size 1X. Photo credit: Eric Berg.

(upper left) F. Tara Weber in a blue and white swimsuit. Size 16W. Photo credit: James E. Weber, III.

(upper right) Nylon/lycra black and white swimsuit with illusion netting around front placket. Daisies are embroidered along the top bustline. Size 24W. Cat Nordling models. Photo credit: Sandie Sabo.

(lower left) Linda Kanzinger enjoying the Columbia River at Roosevelt, Washington. Black one-piece nylon/spandex suit with floral print, size 24W. Photo credit: Terria Caldwell.

(above) Jeri Carmichael celebrates the sun! Two-piece bathing suit. black/shiny gold, 90% nylon, 10% lycra, top size 22/24W; bottom 26/28W.

As we women of size and substance attempt to dress in clothes that make us look and feel attractive in the hot summertime, we are still in a surround of fat-hating people, a society that looks down on fat with disgust. The plus-size experts state emphatically that one solution to this is for us as fat women to be well-groomed and always dress immaculately. They feel this will lessen the prejudice against us, and eventually, people at large will accept us.

I don't agree with this premise.

I think that we as fat women should dress

OUTRAGEOUSLY!

And what do I mean by that?

I mean wearing spaghetti strap halter dresses, tube tops, short shorts, crop tops, two-piece or bikini bathing suits—in other words, **the things** that **everybody else wears** in the **summer.**

CLOTHES FOR BODIES, NOT BODIES FOR CLOTHES.

(right) Kelly Ryan poses with her beach umbrella and black heels in a one-piece black swimsuit, 80% nylon/20% spandex, 20W. Photo credit: Photos by Beth, Mpls, MN.

Bodacious Women Just Lounging Around in their Bathing Suits!

(above) Ashley Taylor Clayton models classic style mallot suit, in black velvet, size 22W. Photo credit: Satu. (below left) Carol L. Gautney, II, in a blue one-piece swim suit, size 20W, 80% nylon, 20% spandex, with 100% nylon lining, wide-strap comfort and black torso-accentuating trim lines. Baseball cap turned sideways completes the outfit.

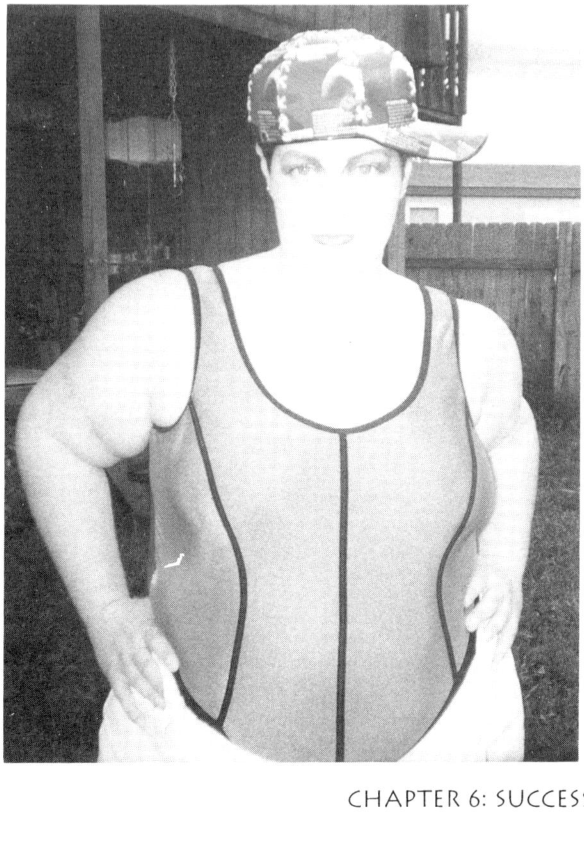

"I'D LOVE TO SEE...

A PLUS-SIZE
BATHING SUIT
IN A STORE
THAT DIDN'T HAVE
BLACK
IN THE DESIGN.

I'D LOVE TO SEE A
SUPERSIZE BATHING
SUIT—

IN A STORE!"

(right) Let's play at the beach! A beachball is enticing, as well as this one-piece skirted black bathing suit with white cording, 80% nylon/20% spandex. Photo credit: Voluptuous Images.

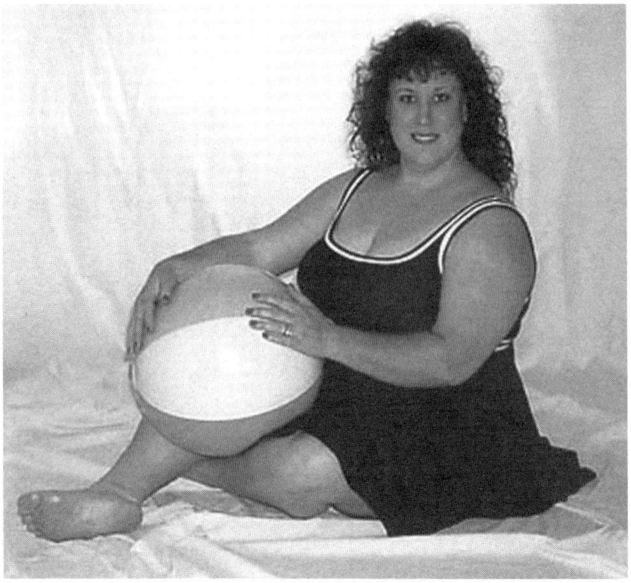

(left) Cathy Bryant is stylewise in her black one-piece swimsuit, with floral print front. With black felt derby hat and coverall. Now get in that Mustang, and rip and roar! Photo credit: Linda Kanzinger.

(right) Gabby Sparapani sports a flashy bathing suit, gold & black with front zipper and headband. 80% nylon/20% spandex, size 22/24W and coordinated top.

(upper right) Cathy Bryant in swimsuit and black knit zippered coverup. A coverup is a graceful way to walk from car to beach, or dash in and out of the convenient store for all those things that go along with "going to the beach". Photo credit: Linda Kanzinger.

COVER-UPS

(above left) Here's a wonderful example of "breaking the rules". Fat women are discouraged from wearing two piece bathing suits. How many do you see hanging in a rack on a store—especially in the supersizes? Here, Jeri Carmichael pleases and inspires us with her gracious presence, showing the beauty of a fat woman's body. Black/shiny gold, 90% nylon, 10% lycra, top size 22/24W; bottom 26/28W.

(lower right) Cat Nordling listening to the soothing sounds of the California ocean. Black flowered print rayon georgette double layer dress over swimsuit. The underlayer is a small floral print, knee length. Attached to the underdress is a lace panel which is visible above the overdress. Overdress is a larger floral print. Size 24W from Daytons. Photo credit: Sandie Sabo.

SIZE-POSITIVE FASHION PRINCIPLES:
SILHOUETTE

"The shape of the silhouette usually complements the shape of the body, but exaggeration is often used to create a special effect or balance and emphasize a part of the body that is a current focus of fashion."

Sharon Lee Tate-*Inside Fashion Design*

"A maxim for a beautiful silhouette is that it neither reveals all nor conceals all of the figure."

Harriet McJimsey-*Art and Fashion in Clothing Selection*

Silhouette is the last basic fashion principle I am going to discuss. The silhouette is the outline of the clothing. Silhouettes for plus and supersize women are based upon the shape of the body, and extend outwards. Today's silhouettes are varied, as clothing design itself is more varied, and the function of specialty clothing (activewear, career wear, formal wear) has widened.

The silhouette is achieved by cutting and manipulating fabric into a certain clothing form. Darts, yokes, collars, sleeves, pockets, fasteners, and fringes can strengthen and support the design theme by harmonizing with the silhouette. These elements supply form to the silhouette.

There are a number of different silhouettes used at various times in history. The three basic silhouettes down through time are:

- **the straight-line or tubular**
- **the curved or bell-shape**
- **the back-draped or bustle**

Most plus and supersize clothing designers favor the **body-skimming silhouette**, in other words, a relaxed fit or relaxed-ease design, which "skims" the plus or supersize body. They also like to use lots of "ease" which is fabric allowance, so there's room to move within the clothing.

"What starts out as a good idea becomes a vicegrip, as the majority of clothing is styled in this way. **Relaxed-ease silhouette** should not be the only choice for the abundant woman."

ACTIVEWEAR

(above right) Exhilerating exercise on the trampoline! Cathy Bryant in her one-piece navy unitard jumps, and Linda Kanzinger catches the action—in mid-air!

(above and previous page) Cathy Bryant wearing herself out on the trampoline! A blue unitard, 90% cotton, 10% spandex, from Lane Bryant, is an example of the natural body silhouette and gives both support and comfort to this bodacious babe! (lower right) Wearing a black and white matching nylon jogging outfit in the midst of a jog, Cathy defers to a photographer. Photo credit: Linda Kanzinger.

ALTERNATE SILHOUETTE TYPOLOGY

The most sensible way to create silhouettes for plus and supersize women is to use each body type as a building block, and build outward. The following material is drawn from the book, *Inside Fashion Design* by Sharon Lee Tate. Beginning with the silhouette that most closely follows the body, she then shows varying degrees where the silhouette moves away from the body.

In her typology, the first silhouette is the **natural body silhouette.** Clothing such as **leotards, body suits, swimwear, dancewear and other exercisewear** all follow the body's shape closely. Look at the photographs above and to the left of Cathy Bryant wearing a unitard, to see an example of the **natural body silhouette.**

The next silhouette described by Tate is the **slim line silhouette.** This shape hugs the body with little air space. **Snug-fitting jeans, any tight clothes, tailored classic clothes, and straight-legged pants** are all slim-line; so are tight sweaters and closely fitted blouses. Look at the photographs on page 46 of Cleacia Foster in jeans and a shirt which illustrate the slim-line silhouette, or of Cheryl Anderson on page 124 in a pair of stretch leggings and a sleeveless knit T-shirt.

A **tailored silhouette** is basically rectangular. **Slim suits, clinging dresses with darts, and shirtwaist dresses with straight skirts** are examples of this category of Tate's. A tailored silhouette will hide a defined waist, so it is better suited to the squarish body shape. Also, this design is restrictive to the body in a way that the natural body silhouette is not. There is less ease of movement. However, with the use of curved lines, the tailored silhouette will work with the curves of the Reubenesque woman. (See Kelly Ryan in the pink suit in Chapt 7, page 132)

Soft dressing, Tate's next category, originates from the natural body silhouette but adds some fullness. The clothing has more ease and uses pleats and gathers to achieve a fuller fit. Usually the fabrics are softer and thinner, whereas natural body silhouettes use stretch fabrics predominantly. **Pleated pants, sweat pants, full dirndl skirts, gathered skirts, and the shift or float with pleats or gathers from the shoulder** are some examples of this category. Soft dressing creates a wide, rectangular silhouette, but it is not stiff like the tailored or slim-line one. There is also ease of movement. (Look at the dresses on page 51 and 136 worn by Myra Turley for examples of soft dressing.)

(left) A playful Kim Caldwell horsing around at Horsethief Butte in the Columbia Gorge. She's wearing a pink T-shirt, XL, black lycra stretch pants, XL, and cross-training shoes. Photo credit: Linda Kanzinger (lower left) Cheryl Anderson enjoying a hike in the Columbia Gorge, in practical outdoor wear including this bright yellow 100% cotton zippered sweatshirt, size XXL. Photo credit: Linda Kanzinger.

Soft dressing is a **moderate silhouette modification**, according to Tate, in that the silhouette comes away from the body in a moderate fashion. Yet it is important to note that there is still a defined waistline and torso. The ease and fullness is in the shoulders, arms, legs, calves. Movement is easier, for the legs and torso are unimpaired. There is more bulk surrounding the hips. Yokes are used to provide ease, as in fuller blouses. Gathers or shirring are also popular.

Tate's next silhouette design uses **extreme silhouette modification**, meaning that the silhouette departs from the body's natural lines quite dramatically. One example is the **shoulder wedge silhouette.** This is a very masculine, or yang, silhouette. **Shoulder pads, shoulder ruffles, and leg-o-mutton sleeves** are several examples of this silhouette. It is most effective when contrasted with a slim lower body silhouette. Another way of enhancing the upper body dominance is through having **very full dolman, raglan, or batwing sleeves.**

Another example of **extreme silhouette modification,** according to Tate, is the **hourglass figure.** In contrast to the shoulder wedge, the hourglass is very feminine, or yin. It follows the "ideal" (or at least ideal in certain times) feminine figure. In general, the top of the design is fitted close to the bodice with full sleeves, and the bottom is also very full. Fitting and padding at the shoulder line and waist reinforces the top of the hourglass, while the bottom of the hourglass is reinforced with decoration on the hemline. See the wedding dresses on page 86-87 for examples of this **hourglass figure silhouette modification.**

Extreme silhouette modification can also occur with Tate's concept of **figure volume**. Figure volume can occur with bulk added to the torso or top of the figure, as in bulky winter jackets made out of wool, or a fur coat. (See photos of myself on page 104-105, 117) In fact, one of the basic reasons for figure volume silhouettes is to add warmth and padding during cold weather. Most thick women "wear an extra sweater" anyway in terms of body fat, and it is fair to say that figure volume occurs naturally in full-bodied women, thus omitting the need to add volume!

Many times this winterwear consists of bulky garments on the top with narrow pants, often stretch pants, to provide ease of movement. **Winter sportswear** is often designed with this silhouette. Other possibilities are: **coats, capes, large shawls, and bulky sweaters** worn with long skirts or pants. These items are made from **wool, leather, thick fabrics such as fur,** and include **quilted clothing**.

A second way of creating a **figure volume silhouette,** according to Tate, is through **layering.** This can be accomplished with heavy or thick fabrics. As mentioned, the heavy fabrics are usually used for winter protection. The emphasis is on the print or texture of the fabric, and the shape of the figure is minimized. Ethnic clothing is one style which uses the layering principle, as it is featured with the mixing of prints, an emphasis on the fabric used, and a minimizing of the body's shape. For Reubenesque women, a figure volume silhouette is often compatible with the woman's shape, providing a harmony between silhouette and body shape.

In warm climates and summer weather, this

(above) Let's play ball! Denim jeans and 100% cotton shirt with baseball and bat. Photo credit: Voluptuous Images. (below) Equestrienne Lynne Shaw on Kioya, an Appaloosa gelding from Crimson Acres Farm, Orange, MA. She's wearing a white cotton turtleneck, size 2X, lavender stretch stirrup pants, 22W, black angle boots with silver tips, and black cotton best with multicolored beads and embroidery, size 3X. Photo credit: Crimson Acres Farm, Orange, MA.

layered look can be used successfully with very lightweight fabrics, such as lightweight cottons, linens, rayons, and cotton gauze. This has been a popular summer look, with the soft draping of the figure. **Draped shawls and capes** can be worn over pants. **Wide-leg pants,** such as **harem or jodhpurs,** are very successful when made in lightweight soft fabrics. A lot of ease is added to the pattern to increase the volume of the figure, yet, with the use of belting, the figure does not have to be shapeless.

One very successful example of this style is seen in the book *Breaking All The Rules* (Nancy Roberts). She shows an example of an outfit with layers of clothing in a soft light fabric: pants, then a skirt, with a wide sash-waistband; a button-down shirt, over this a wide duster, and finally over this a long vest, plus a fringed scarf wrapped around the neck. Everything is in the same stripe fabric, a very lightweight, light textured fabric, and the effect is that of a very successful look!

OTHER SILHOUETTE IDEAS

The popular book, *The Lane Bryant Fashion Math Make-Over* by Lane Bryant, presents several silhouette ideas. They include: **Fit-and-Flare, Long-over-Flare, and Long-over-Lean.**

• **Fit-and-Flare** is fitted on the top and flares out. It is accomplished with a wide belt. A shirtwaist dress with a gathered or pleated skirt is a good example. This is a good silhouette for the Pear, Venus, SuperPear or SuperVenus.

• **Long-over-Flare** is popular, especially with squarish shapes such as Reubenesque, Tall Reubenesque, and those without a waist, such as Apple. A long tunic or sweater worn with a pleated short skirt that "kicks out" is one example.

• **Long-over-Lean** is a popular silhouette, with straight-line clothing such as one-piece dresses, sweaters and jeans, or straight skirts. Again, this silhouette works better on a squarish rather than a curvy figure. Tall Reubenesque and Juno also have the height which helps with that vertical line requirement!

Two other silhouettes look balanced to the eye. These are **Long-over-Short,** and **Short-over-Long.**

• **Long-over-Short** is part of the previously mentioned **Long-over-Flare,** with the obvious difference. Examples of **Long-over-Short** include a big shirt with a miniskirt or a long T-shirt over short shorts. It's one of my favorite silhouettes!

• **Short-over-Long** would include a straight chemise dress with an overbodice. This is a popular style currently.

(right) Alaska fishing trip is a success— in a nylon quilted jacket, 22W, and jeans and T-shirt. Cathy Bryant grins as the halibut stares. Photo credit: Rob Bryant.

(above left) Author enjoying a ski trip at Mt Hood near her home of Portland, OR. Crocheted cap and matching crocheted leggings, designed and made by the author, nylon shell pants, size 20W, T-shirts, size 22W, and men's blue pullover sweater, XXL.

(above right) This Norwegian likes to ski! Author in matching handknit sweater and leggings, designed and made by the author; wool Navy pants, men's XL, in the Blue Mountains of Oregon.

(left) Let's go boating! Cathy Bryant anticipating a full day of fun in the sun, wearing comfortable white strap sandals, bluejean shortalls, with white tee. Now all she needs is some sunscreen! Photo credit: Linda Kanzinger

WORK CLOTHES: HARD HATS, FIREFIGHTERS, CARPENTRY, UNIFORMS, AND OTHER NONTRADITIONAL OUTFITS

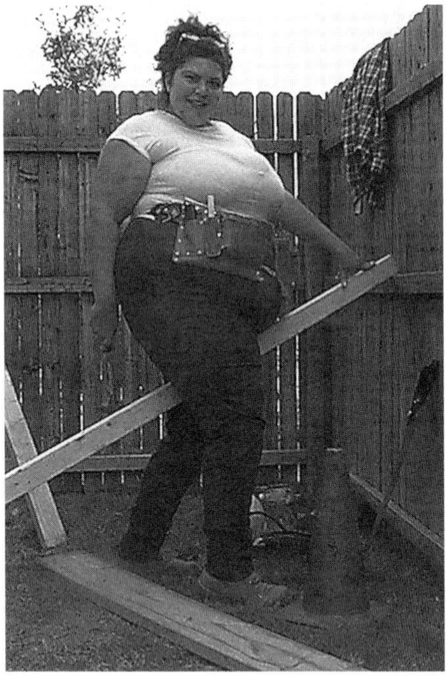

above left) It takes a big woman to do a big job! Cleacia Foster is up to the task in a man's white T-shirt, XL, bluejeans, 22/24W, and leather carpenter's belt.

((below left) Linda Kanzinger's proud of learning how to use her chainsaw! She's in the woods at Timber Valley, wearing a blue man's XL sweater and size 20W bluejeans. Leather boots are a necessity! (right) Kim Caldwell's ready for lunch! No more site inspection for her. She's attired in a safety helmet, flowered nylon zippered jacket, 18W, black cotton/lycra stretch pants, XL, boots, shades, and lunch basket.

Now, with the obvious variations in these shapes, it is logical to follow that certain clothing designs will look better on certain shapes than on others. And, some designs would be inappropriate for a particular shape, but enhance another. This is why it isn't possible to say exactly that certain styles work for plus and supersize women, generically, because there are too many different types of plus and supersize women's shapes.

However, now that you are aware of the **principles** of silhouette, it will be easier for you to identify a particular outfit as to which type of silhouette it is —and thus to understand why certain types of clothes look better on you than others. At least, this is my hope! Today's silhouettes are varied, as clothing design is more varied and the function of specialty clothing (activewear, career wear, formal wear) has widened.

(right) Firefighter Lynne Shaw has what it takes to do the job! NFPA (National Fire Protection Association) certified turnout coat, bunkerpants with suspenders, helmet with face shield, fire boots and fire gloves. A police officer at the scene shot this photo right after she finished fighting the fire. Photo credit: Millbury Police Department.

HOW TO 'READ' A GARMENT OR PATTERN FOR ITS' FASHION PRINCIPLES IN A SIZE-POSITIVE WAY

Now that you've learned body types, and the basics of fashion principles, including silhouettes, as well as how silhouettes translate outward into a variety of clothing styles, it's very easy to learn how to "read" a garment or pattern that fits for your type.

There are a few simple guidelines that can be followed:

1 Choose a focal point on your body that you want to emphasize and look for clothing designs which emphasize that.

For example, if you want to **emphasize your waist,** look for:

- **A sweater-dress with a wide ribbing waistband in the middle**

• A pleated or gathered skirt with a wide waistband
• A fitted top or jacket with many waistline darts and a small peplum

What about **emphasizing your bust?** Look for:

• A low-cut V-line silk blouse to be worn under a suit jacket and skirt
• A princess-line dress in a knit with a low-cut neckline
• An off-the-shoulder evening dress with a push-up bra underneath

2 Remember which body shapes will not work well with certain clothing shapes because of structural disaffinity:

A **Pear** or a **Superpear** will not look good in a tailored suit with straight-cut blazer and skirt because there is an underlying disaffinity due to the face that the **Pear** is a rounded shape and the suit is a rectangular shape.

COATS AND OUTERWEAR

(Upper right) Sharon Klose wearing a long wool coat by Sue Brett, size 32W, with neck scarf. Photo credit: Perri Neri. (Below left) Classy and elegant, Emanon models a faux fur winter coat with faux fur hat, polypropylene fabric, size XL. Photo credit: Vic Toliva, Detroit, MI.

(upper left) Sharon Klose models a rain/all weather coat. Purple with fuchsia accents by CST Collection in size 32W. Photo credit: Perri Neri. (right) Cathy Bryant in long wool black/grey/ white zebra stripe coat. Photo credit: Linda Kanzinger

(lower left) Kim Caldwell modeling a long black wool winter coat with princess lines. Photo credit: Phyllis Caldwell.

3 Choose an emphasis or focal point on your body that you want to de-emphasize, and then look for a flattering silhouette.

For example, if you are a **Pear** and you want to de-emphasize your hips you could:

- **Wear a pleated or gathered skirt made from a moderately stiff fabric— a cotton or linen, for example**

A **Juno** or **Scallop** might want to de-emphasize their midriff, waist, stomach, and abdomen. They could:

- **Wear any number of silhouettes which drape from the shoulder and flow down. Floats and shifts with pleats or gathers on the shoulder line are one popular style**

WEARABLE ART: HANDCRAFTED, HAND-PAINTED OR DYED, KNIT, CROCHETED, WOVEN, OR PATCHWORK CLOTHING

(above) Blue and purple tie-dye T-shirt, size L, and hand-dyed silk-screened silk scarf with patterns of huckleberries. Black cotton man's pants, size XL. Worn by the author as she cuts bamboo.

- Another style features peplums and diagonal lines across the midriff area. The emphasis of the silhouette is either on the shoulder or drapes diagonally across the center of the garment

A **Venus** or **Supervenus** might want to de-emphasize her bustline one time, and emphasize it another time.

To emphasize:

- Wear tight sweaters, particularly in lighter weight fabrics, both cotton, wool, and acrylic. Also cotton or synthetic tank and other knit tops Wear wide belts with clothing to emphasize bustline

To De-Emphasize:

- Wear stiffer fabrics, such as medium-weight cotton or linen, for blouses. For thinner fabrics—silks, acetates, synthetics, or rayon, wear a design with a front tie or a pleated front, anything that will minimize the bustline

THE MORE WE LOOK AT OURSELVES AND EACH OTHER IN CLOTHING,

THE MORE DESIGNERS DESIGN FOR PLUS AND SUPERSIZE WOMEN,

THE MORE WE GET AWAY FROM COMPARING HOW WE LOOK IN A PARTICULAR OUTFIT WITH HOW A TALL SKINNY MODEL LOOKS IN THE SAME PARTICULAR TYPE OF CLOTHING,

THE MORE OUR OPTIONS EXPAND,

AS WE ARE ABLE TO APPRECIATE

OUR PARTICULAR BODY SHAPE

AND HOW WE LOOK IN CLOTHES!

A person usually likes to alternate between a variety of images and it is truly up to us to choose what part of our bodies we want to feature, and what "look" we want to wear today. Although most people have preferences for what looks best on them, it is helpful to experiment with different looks on occasion. It's amazing how many different kinds of clothes look good on us now that we have the opportunity!

NEW SIZE-POSITIVE FASHION PRINCIPLES

The following ideas are based on three of my precepts as well as introducing some new size-positive fashion principles for the fat woman. Let's review the precepts.

1 EVERY BODY IS OK.

2 CLOTHES NEED TO BE DESIGNED FOR THE BODY, RATHER THAN THE BODY DESIGNED FOR THE CLOTHING.

3 NO PARTS OF YOUR BODY ARE "GOOD", OR" BAD". YOU CAN CHOOSE TO EMPHASIZE OR DE-EMPHASIZE ANY PART OF YOUR BODY THROUGH HOW YOU WEAR YOUR CLOTHES.

Here are more size-positive fashion principles that I will go into much more depth in a following book on clothing for plus and supersize women.

4 THE PRINCIPLE OF THE FLUIDITY OF KNIT **means that we as fat women can wear knits! Knits have a fluidity that work well with the size and substance of fat bodies. It gives, it springs back, it stretches over our curves.**

5 THE PRINCIPLE OF DRAPED CLOTHING. **Draped clothing works very well on the supersize body. Look at the body shape as a sculpture. Draping fabric into clothing shapes makes much more sense than trying to design for 3D bodies with 2D thinking!**

6 DESIGN OF THE BODY DOMINANT/ DESIGN OF THE CLOTHES DOMINANT **means sometimes the design of the clothing is the dominant feature, and your body is the backdrop. Other times your body is the centerpiece, and the clothing is barely an accessory!**

7 THE COLOR PRINCIPLE. **Wear colors that lift and clarify your image.**

8 CHOOSE YOUR LINES. **This means that you sometimes choose horizontal lines. Don't always be locked into focusing on the vertical line. Enjoy curved lines and the excitement of diagonals.**

9 LET YOUR CLOTHES RESHAPE YOUR NATURAL BALANCE—SOMETIMES. **This means sometimes using the fashion principles of balance and proportion to approximate the "ideal figure".**

(below right) An example of wearable art worn by Sharon Klose. "Allison-Che" turquoise embroidered vest, size 34W, top, and pants. A sweetly romantic look. Photo credit: Perri Neri.

10 LET YOUR CLOTHES REFLECT YOUR NATURAL BALANCE—OTHER TIMES. **This means going with your body! Wearing things which reveal your natural balance, not trying to balance to the proportions of the "ideal figure".**

11 THE PRINCIPLE OF FABRIC SIMPLY MEANS **how important the choice of fabric is in a garment. It's not just fine-quality fabrics, although that helps, but it is the co-ordination of the fabric to the style of the garment, and how that interacts with the body.**

And here are some final ideas and tips for dressing with size-positive style!

12 YOU CAN COORDINATE THE CLOTHING STYLE WITH THE STYLE OF A PORTION OF THE BODY SHAPE. **For example, if a Pear's lower body is succulent and sexy, you can choose a clothing design where the lower portion of the design reveals the voluptuousness of the shape.**

13 PLEATS AND GATHERS CREATE AN ANGLE TO THE FABRIC. **In other words, the fabric does not lay flat, but rather is set at an angle. Pleats and gathers are good clothing detail lines to have at points in the body shape where one wants to minimize the original body shape.**

14 ASK YOURSELF: WHERE IS THE FOCAL POINT OF THIS CLOTHING? **Then, compare the focal point of the clothing with the part of the body shape which you wish to emphasize in this particular design. A Venus, for example, can look for clothing which emphasizes 1) the hourglass silhouette 2) the waistline 3) the bosom.**

15 REMEMBER AS WELL, ASK YOURSELF—WHAT DO I WANT TO EMPHASIZE IN MY BODY SHAPE? THIS IS A MATTER OF CHOICE, AND IT CAN CHANGE. **At one time, I may wish to emphasize a "safe" part of my body—ie a part that I know is acceptable to others. Other times I may want to be daring and reveal body shapes that usually I keep covered.**

(above) A swirl of color in the green Oregon forest. Cheryl Anderson walks and ponders the beauty in a tie-dye sleeveless V-neck cotton shirt, XL, with black cotton/lycra leggings and cross-training shoes. Photo credit: John L. Smith

(above left) Another example of wearable art is quilted clothing. Marilyn Webb, of Toronto, Kansas, models her hand-made quilted light blue vest with dirndl skirt.

(above right) Striped quilted vest, designed, made and modeled by Marilyn Webb. Worn with blue-jeans.

(above left and right) Two views of a handmade colorful quilted jacket designed, made, and modeled by Marilyn Webb. Bright fuchsia pink with turquoise print fabric, with diagonal stripes and diamond quilt shapes.

(above) Handcrafted clothing for large women. Cardigan type sweater made by Wanda S. Meyer of Sioux City, IA, one piece construction, ostrich-plume stitch, metal buttons, 100% cotton slubbed yarn. Size 44-48.

(below left) Handknit sweater by Wanda S. Meyer. Circular construction, 50% cotton/ 50% wool/ 3/4 length sleeves. Size 44-48.

(below right) Handknit sweater made by Wanda S. Meyer of seamless construct-ion, tunic length, full length sleeves, splits at sides, saddle shoulders, 100% wool. Size 44-48.

ACCESSORIES:
HATS, SCARVES, GLOVES, HOSIERY, PURSES, SHOES

(above) Fuchsia colored net scarf wraps and shapes Emanon in an elegant manner. Photo credit: Vic Toliva.

(above) Linda Kanzinger beaming as she wears her favorite 100% rayon woven multicolored scarf with black fringe. Red, pink, green, line green, yellow, orange, and purple stripes. (below) Cathy Bryant tips her lace and flowered broad-brimmed straw hat. Photo credit: Linda Kanzinger.

(above) A fuchsia and light baby pink long neck scarf provides a dramatic accent to Andrea E. Cipala's navy blue suit.

(below) A favorite red straw hat helps protect from the sun.

(above) A comfortable straw Panama hat with a ribbon circled round the brim!

(above and below) A black wool fedora hat.

(above) One can accessorize as well with hair ornaments, as shown by Cheryl Anderson wearing her thick lush hair in a pony tail with a floral shaped fabric barrette. Photo credit: Linda Kanzinger.

(below) Another style of Panama hat worn by Delores Young. Photo credit: Kim Caldwell.

More hats modeled by Cathy Bryant!

7

STYLES AND ARCHETYPES

"STYLE IS THE CLOTHES—
PLUS YOUR BODY
PLUS YOUR CREATIVITY—
THEN PUTTING IT ALL TOGETHER!"

Linda Kanzinger *Size-Positive Style!*

"Although every one can wear classic clothes, this look does not suit everyone equally. A woman with a dramatic face or body will look boring in classic clothes, while a voluptuous, romantic woman will look severe."

Carole Jackson-*Color Me Beautiful*

HISTORICAL PERSPECTIVE ON STYLES

Many people have found the concept of typologies of style very useful. Emily Cho, in her 1986 book *It's You*, first set forth the idea that people could, and did dress in many differing styles. In other words, they just didn't have one style that they wore all the time. And, these various styles could be "typed", thus the origin of the word "typology."

Different styles could be appropriate for different situations, but, based on their personality, most people fell into one or two basic types. Since Cho first presented her ideas, many other books include similar information. These include: *Color Me Beautiful* by Carole Jackson, *Clothe Your Spirit* by Jennifer Robin, *Clothes Sense* by Barbara Werland and Leslie Wood, *Universal Style* by Alyce Parsons and Diane Parente, *Always in Style* by Doris Poosner, and *Conservative Chic* by Amelia Fatt. Perhaps some of these writers were inspired by Cho's typology of styles.

GENERAL FASHION BOOKS

Cho's typology , in *It's You*, includes:

- **Sporty/Casual**
- **Classic/Elegant**
- **Dramatic/Exotic**
- **Romantic/Feminine**
- **Arty/Offbeat**
- **Sexy/Alluring**

In *Metamorphosis*, David Kibbe expands on her concept, using the term "image identity", but the basic gist is the same: a set of questions helping the woman to find her identity or personality type, and then correlating that with the external image. Kibbe's categories are:

- **Dramatic**
- **Romantic**
- **Classic**
- **Natural**
- **Gamine**

He also has subcategories:

- **Dramatic Classic**
- **Soft Dramatic**
- **Theatrical Romantic**
- **Soft Classic**
- **Flamboyant Natural**
- **Soft Natural**
- **Flamboyant Gamine**
- **Soft Gamine**

Janet Wallach, in her book *Looks That Work*, uses:

- **Sophisticated**
- **Romantic**
- **Sporty**
- **Classic**
- **Daring**

Another important fashion writer, Leah Feldon, in her book *Dress Like a Million*, breaks the styles into five broad categories which are based on fashion styles alone. They are:

- **Bas Couture**
- **MTV Chic**
- **Le Sportif Motif**
- **Classic Chic**
- **Yeeps**

She also describes four different personality styles:

- **Active**
- **Natural and Basic**
- **Chic and Feminine**
- **Coquettish**

Bas Couture means "dressing down". Its wearers don a look of studied casualness, with a blend of eras. **MTV Chic** is directly inspired from MTV fashion styles: lots of black, skintight spandex, Lycra, leather, and lace. **Le Sportif Motif** is a French sounding way of describing running around in activewear. **Classic Chic** means staying with traditional concepts in fashion—nothing is experimental or faddish. **Yeeps** is her word to describe Young Environmentally Enlightened Professionals. Brand names include LL Bean, Eddie Bauer and Patagonia. Natural fabrics in earth tones, and environmentally friendly textile processes are preferred.

"AS HAS BEEN POINTED OUT MANY TIMES BEFORE, AS **WOMEN GAIN** MORE **POWER** IN THE OUTSIDE WORLD, **FASHION PRESENTS IMAGES** THAT CONFORM MORE AND MORE TO **MEN S BODIES:** SHOULDER WEDGE SHAPE, **BOYISH HIPS, FLAT CHESTS.**

THIS IS NO COINCIDENCE, BUT RATHER AN ATTEMPT

TO **DENIGRATE** WOMANLINESS— **WOMAN'S SHAPE.**"

PLUS-SIZE FASHION BOOKS

Some, but not all plus-size fashion writers include categories of styles. Pivotal works which omit this include *Breaking All the Rules*-Nancy Roberts, *Life is Not a Dress Size*-Rita Farro, and *The Triumph of Individual Style*-Carla Mason Mathis and Helen Villa Connor. However, in *Style is Not a Size,* Hara Marano includes:

- **Classic**
- **Romantic**
- **The Femme Fatale**
- **Gamine or Ingenue**
- **Natural**

The Lane Bryant Fashion Math Make-Over includes:

- **Dramatic**
- **Romantic**
- **Classic**
- **Casual**

Suzan Nanfeldt, in *Plus Style: The Plus Size Guide to Looking Great*, includes:

- **Natural/Sporty**
- **Elegant/Classic**
- **Romantic/Feminine**
- **Glamorous/Sexy**
- **Dramatic/Artistic**

As you can see, the most common and familiar to all of these writers are **Classic, Romantic, Dramatic, Sporty, and Sexy.**

(above right) Step out in style! Teresa Marie Metcalfe-Johnson certainly does, with an elegant sashay— a straw hat tops the classy outfit of this one-piece black dress with polka dot cuffs and flounced hem. Top is cotton spandex with sheer layers below, size 3X, by Astarte Woman. Photo credit: Satu. (right) Sexy is as sexy gets. How about a black spaghetti strap slipdress with gold sparkles worn out on the town? Tatoos complete the ensemble. Size 26/28W. Cleacia Foster models. Photo credit: Skip Orlando.

Examples of some of the more popular fashion styles: (upper left) Emanon models the clean lines of the classic look, in a checkered wool suit with white collar and cuffs, size 20W. Photo credit: Vic Toliva.

(upper right) Sherry Lynette walks in stride along the New Mexico stucco in a bone colored silk/cotton blend V neck summer sweater, size 18/20 , with front-pleated khaki linen pants, thigh length, with zipper front and side pockets. size 20— an example of the natural look. Photo credit: © Monico Candelaria/Photographer.

(lower left) A romantic and feminine look in a soft pink suit with peplum, 50% rayon/50% polyester, size 20W. Both the color and style of the suit adds to its' romantic appeal, not to mention the pretty red-head wearing it! Kelly Ryan models. Photo credit: Jim Woosley @ Jim Woosley Photograph, Mpls, MN.

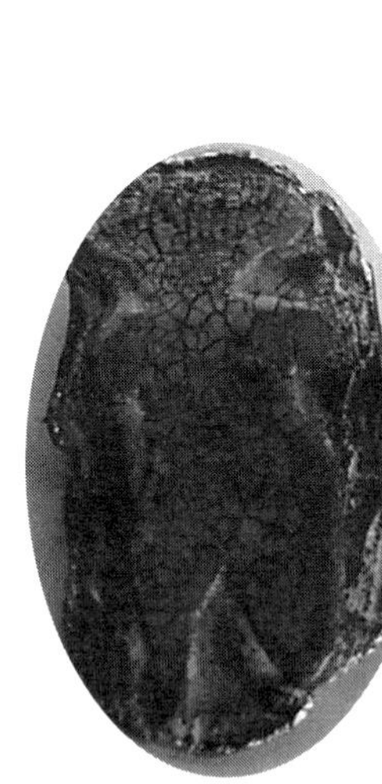

(above) "Crackle Pin" - Kim Caldwell. 2"x3". Rubber stamped image from Her Rubber of goddess figure, stamped onto Sculpty clay, overlaid with crackle varnish, outlined with gold pen. © 1999 by Kim Caldwell. Photo credit: Linda Kanzinger.

STYLES TODAY

Of course, none of these regular fashion books are considering the voluptuous woman as part of their audience. We as plus-size women need to emphasize the womanliness of our bodies. We are women. We are curvaceous, voluptuous, soft, desirable, pretty. Part of woman-hating is hating womanly bodies. As has been pointed out many times before, as women gain more power in the outside world, fashion presents images that conform more and more to men's bodies: shoulder wedge shape, boyish hips, flat chests. This is no coincidence, but rather an attempt to denigrate womanliness: woman's shape.

Nevertheless, studying these various typologies can be very useful, as the real woman can use the basic concepts, and some of the plus-size fashion books are fairly size-positive. It helps us to delineate which style or styles we are most comfortable with. It also helps us to explore new styles and ways of dressing. We can learn to dress in many different styles: for example, I have learned to put outfits together more creatively.

The women's movement has helped to loosen the dictates of the fashion industry as to what we "should" wear. There is a positive trend today regarding clothes and fashion, as women are no longer bowing to the dictates of fashion whims. "This season's fashion" as a uniform is no longer necessary, as it once was twenty-five years ago.

In those days, a certain look was "in", and it didn't matter how poorly an individual woman would look in "it". Conformity was strong enough that wearing the latest look was deemed more important than whether or not you looked foolish in the latest look!

"WE AS PLUS-SIZE AND SUPERSIZE WOMEN NEED TO EMPHASIZE THE WOMANLINESS OF OUR BODIES.

WE ARE WOMEN.

WE ARE CURVACEOUS, VOLUPTUOUS, SOFT, DESIRABLE, PRETTY.

PART OF WOMAN-HATING IS

HATING WOMANLY BODIES."

(Above) With fresh-faced Midwestern appeal, Cheryl Anderson exemplifies the Confident/Active style in a pale yellow 100% cotton swing shirt, size XL. Photo credit: John L. Smith. (below) Emanon models a layered outfit of silver washable silk slacks, top and jacket with silver leather sandals. Dressy, yet with that sand-washed appeal. Size 24W. Photo credit: Vic Toliva, Detroit, MI.

I credit the young women of today of pushing the concept of clothes and fashion even further into an arena of freedom and choice. Young women, for the most part, have completely thrown off the strictures of the past, and wear whatever they want! They combine clothes in most interesting fashions. Hemlines are long to mini. Plus size young women wear miniskirts, which I think is entirely appropriate.

It is refreshing to see women claim fashion as their own, rather than having it be dictated to them.

One reason why the fashion industry has been forced to respond to what women want, rather than women responding to what the fashion industry wants them to want, is that women's lives are more complex. We play out more complex roles, and therefore we need more variety in our clothing. We need clothes for more occasions—not a problem for us clothes-lovers! The more, the merrier! Another reason is that many adult women are now a part of the fashion industry, and thus influence its direction.

Therefore, a number of books on fashion and style are emphasizing personal style rather than conscious conformity. In fact, the changes in our modern world as regards woman's roles has likely brought about this emphasis on the individual and the personal, rather than the mass. This makes dressing or "looking good" more complex, but ultimately more rewarding, as a person can find her own unique style. Clothing can be a visual language, rather than a way of conformity.

SIZE -POSITIVE STYLE

Size Positive Style needs new names. I propose

- **Confident/Active**
- **Dramatic/HeadTurner**
- **Curvy/Sexy**
- **Classic/Career**
- **Soft/Feminine**
- **Artistic/Multiethnic**

SIZE-POSITIVE STYLE: CONFIDENT/ACTIVE

CONFIDENT/ACTIVE as the name implies, requires that the plus and supersize woman has a confident personality which allows her to wear non-confining clothes, revealing her body and allowing her to move. At least 50% of the clothing manufactured today is sportswear or casual wear, and a large number of plus and supersize clothing presently available fits into the **Confident/Active** style. Other writers call this style **Sporty, Natural, or Casual.**

The **Confident** part of the style is wearing clothes that are no-nonsense, even a slightly tailored sportswear look. Natural fibers and colors give ease of movement and a look of assertive confidence. It also includes more traditional sportswear looks such as plaids and a shirtwaist shirt. This is for the more formal look of **Confident/Active.** The relaxed look in **Active** include traditionally labeled activewear as well as outfits such as shorts and summer tops.

Some ideas in the **Confident** part for the plus and supersize women include:

Blazers
Pleated pants
Shirtwaist cotton dress
Plaids, tweeds, checks
Natural fibers, such as linens, cottons, rayons
Natural colors: off-whites, earthtones
Relaxed fit jackets
Bluejean shorts, shirts, jumpers, and jeans
Long loose-fit knit sweaters, both pull-over and cardigan
Corduroy jumpers
Sandals

And in the **Active** part of the style:

Leotards, unitards
Stirrup pants, leggings
Bicycle pants and shorts
Sports bras
Long-sleeved fleece tops
T-shirts, sweatshirts, and shorts
Cotton big shirts

Examples of Confident/Active (upper right) Cleacia Foster relaxes outdoors in the sunshine wearing a light gray acrylic blend sweater, size 26/28W, with black jeans, size 22/24W. Photo credit: Skip Orlando. (right) Tara Weber's cruisin' in a coordinated outfit of natural colors. Ecru striped pants, ecru camp shirt, white T, and straw sandals. Size 14/16W. Photo credit: Michael Gomez.

Some of the motifs within this style include:

- **The Cotton Look**
- **The Denim Look**

SIZE-POSITIVE STYLE: DRAMATIC/ HEADTURNING

(Above) Andrea Hall wows 'em in her dressy dramatic outfit of front-button off-white acetate/rayon shirt with stand-up collar, size 26/28W, with black tencel pants, size 22/24W, a zebra print scarf, and platform shoes. (below) Myra Turley glows in a rayon mauve taupe dusty rose print dress, size 5, from Magical Creations, of Portland, OR. Photo credit on both: Linda Kanzinger.

DRAMATIC/HEADTURNING is a style for the extroverted bodacious woman with a flair for the dramatic. She wants to be noticed via her style and unique way of dressing. She wants to "make an entrance" when she enters a room, and for this reason, she dresses in a unique way that creates an impression.

Of course, most fat women are noticed, whether we like it or not. We are going to be receiving attention anyway, so even if we don't have a dramatic personality to start with, we may decide to adopt a new persona. We can turn the negative stare into positive admiration!

To do so, **Dramatic/Headturning** takes advantage of her large body as a "canvas" upon which she drapes interesting textures and colors for spectacular effect! She is highly aware of style, of what is "in" and what is not. She usually does not follow the crowd, but picks and chooses motifs that she can then create into her own "signature style". Each piece will enhance her "signature", and she will wear clothing for years and years, regardless of whether or not they are "in style".

Dramatic/Headturning is very purposeful in choosing her wardrobe. In general, she has few clothes, because she shops very intentionally. Every piece has to be a statement. Solid colors predominate, as they are the backdrop for various "statement pieces", ie accessories such as jewelry, scarves, hats.

Dramatic/Headturning is especially exciting on a tall plus-size woman, a Juno, for example, or a Tall Reubenesque or a SuperReubenesque. We flaunt what we've got! We dress to be seen. We dress to make an impact—to show our curves in big splashy prints that we can carry because we're big enough not to be dwarfed by a big showy fabric or a bold showy concept! All the tall supersize women, especially, have a larger "canvas" on which to play out design and color. (See Myra Turley's outfits on page 136-137)

Dramatic chevron stripe shows off this empire waist, rayon Egyptian print evening dress of black/gold/ brown/ and burnt orange. From Magical Creations, in Portland, OR. Myra Turley does the honors! Size XL-32. Photo credit: Linda Kanzinger.

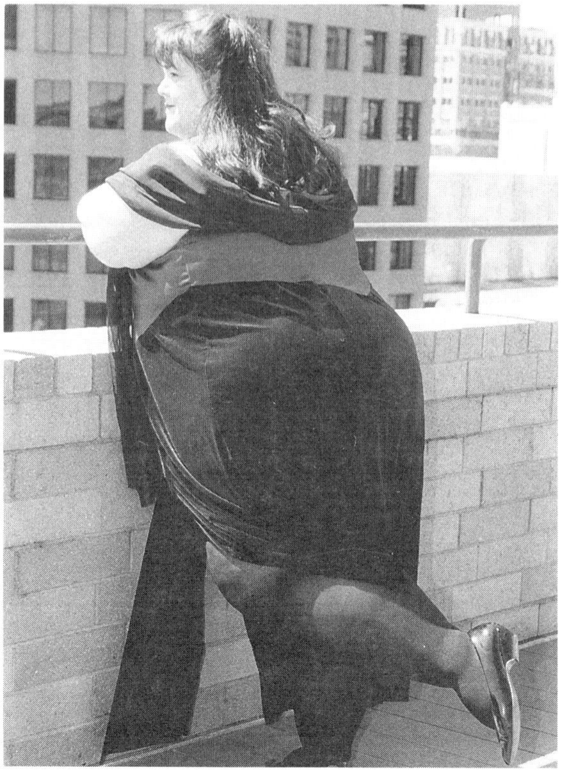

A dramatic look in plum with thigh-high slits and a black chiffon shawl. Cat Nordling designed and models this square neck poly/ satin & rayon/Lycra stretch velvet dress. Black stockings and strappy shoes enhance, entice! Size 32W. Photo credit: Staci Gilbert.

Because we large women have been told for so long to wear dark colors "to make us look smaller" or to cause us to "disappear into the background", I feel it is poetic justice for us to cultivate a style which intentionally reveals us. I find it refreshing to see thick women "letting go" and getting down!

Dramatic/Headturning also is able to handle any attention or remarks that come her way from dressing in this style. As you can no doubt tell, I feel that this typology is one that "breaks all the rules, and it's about time!"

Fabrics and colors for this type include:

Bright solid colors
Big bold unusual patterns
Fabric with novel, unique textures
Dark colors, black predominates
Rich exotic colors: blacks, silvers, purples
Bold prints, including polka dots
Gold, silver, and metallic fabrics
Design details in the style
Well-fitted clothing

and the clothing includes:

Big hats
Oversize and swing jackets
Long skirts: tulip, trumpet, wrap , slit
Brightly patterned scarf
which is the focal point of the outfit
Unique bold jewelry
Glitz and glitter: beaded fabrics using
rhinestones, cabachons, pearls

DRAMATIC/HEAD-TURNING

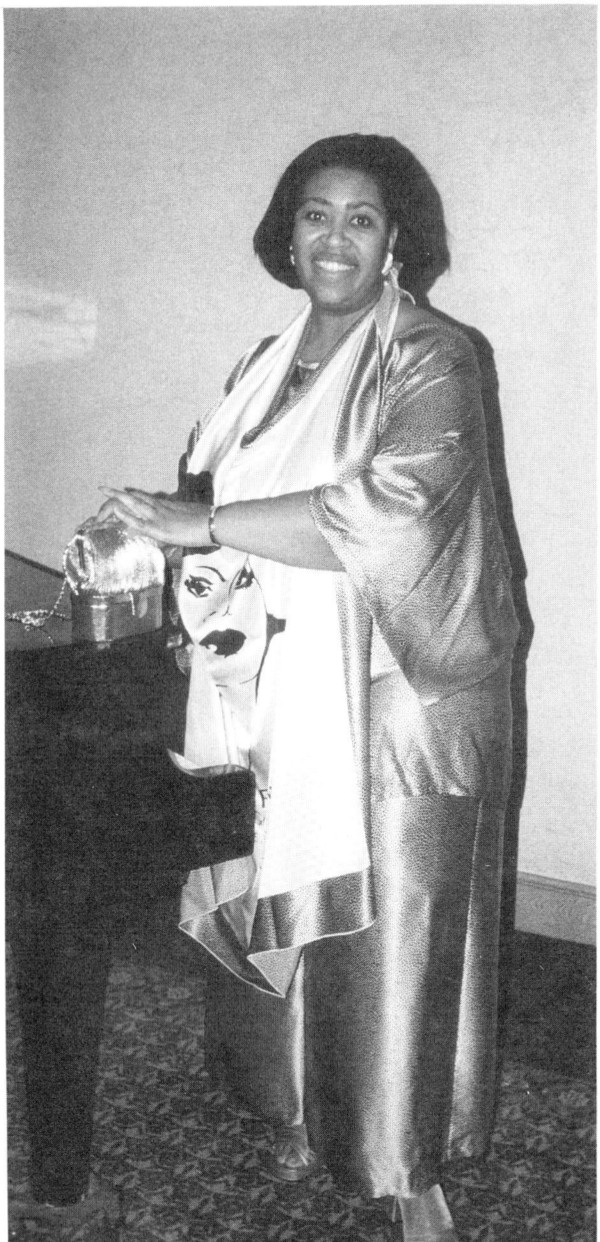

(Above left) Heads will turn when Brenda J. Jones walks in the room wearing this glittery gorgeous outfit! A gold and cream dress with cream-colored scarf with face image and gold border. This is a wonderful example of dramatic elegance. Photo credit: Kim Caldwell.

(above right) What more dramatic statement than dashing off in this off-white wide-lapelled leather blazer ,(XL) along with cream colored slacks, 20W, and leather T-strap silver sandals. A long brown rayon scarf (one size) provides a contrasting accent piece. Emanon is the classy model! Photo credit: Vic Toliva, Detroit, MI.

(above) Elegance exudes from this gold African print suit. 100% cotton with front button gold placket, and gold edging along the blazer, with a long straight skirt. From the African Village, "one size fits most". Andrea Hall does the honors, in Juanita Donaldson's "leopard room". Photo credit: Linda Kanzinger.

(above) A perfect example of Curvy/Sexy: Cleacia Foster models a lacy black bra, size 46DD, with a purple shirt 22/24W, a nylon/lycra blend, from Lane Bryant. (Below) Popular "catsuit" in black cotton interlock, size 5X, with black platform shoes. Cleacia Foster models. Photo credit on both: Skip Orlando.

SIZE-POSITIVE STYLE: CURVY/ SEXY

When I first researched this section, I came to a blank when trying to give lots of examples of sexy clothing for fat women. Luckily, I have many examples now!

CURVY/SEXY is a look, a pose, an attitude. It's the accoutrements: lingerie on the bear skin robe—the jaunt of the hip in tight-fitting clothes— cleavage. It's how you feel about your body— and what you show.

Well, one thing about us bodacious women is that we have curves. Curvy, curvaceous, substantial, ample— curves. So curvy women are sexy women. And we dress to show our curves!

We've got substance. We jiggle, our curves wiggle. We move! So we wear layered sheaths of light-weight fabrics that glimmer and dance along with us. We wear lycra-spandex knits that give us support and stretch at the same time, so we can move. Movement is the message, movement and sexy and curves.

Curvy/Sexy's theme is "fashion is secondary to cling". She is into revealing her body, and uses intense vibrant colors, body-revealing silhouettes, and clingy fabrics to accomplish this end. She uses clothing to make a **body** statement rather than a **fashion** statement. For a plus and especially a supersize woman, this takes a high amount of confidence, but more and more big women are claiming their right to dress, and be, sexy.

Favorite styles include tops with plunging necklines— to reveal cleavage; tight sweaters —to highlight a large bosom; tight short skirts and miniskirts —to reveal big hips, thighs, and rear, and high heels and strappy sandals. She also prefers skirts to pants, so she can show her legs. She also prefers fit to color, and stays away from prints since pure colors reveal her body more easily.

Fabrics, colors, and clothing details include:

Intense vibrant colors, especially

Reds, fuchsias, bright yellows and oranges
See-through fabrics such as loose weaves and netting
Clingy stretchy fabrics such as knits, jerseys, thin silks, satins, tencel rayon
Leather, faux leather, crushed suedes, esp in black, silver, gold
Plunging necklines to reveal cleavage

Clothing examples include:

Low-cut clingy sweater with very tight pants
Leather miniskirt with high heel boots
See-through top with sexy lace bra or camisole underneath
Form-fitting sheath dress
Straight skirts with a side or a back slit

Other embellishments for the **CURVY/SEXY** look include:

Tattoos
Long acrylic nails
Patterned hosiery, fishnet stockings
Seamed silk stockings
High to very high heels

✓ACCENT PLUS-SIZE: Look for wide belts to emphasize the curvy figure of the Venus shape.

✓ACCENT SUPERSIZE: Wide crushy belts to emphasize the curvy figure of SuperVenus; tight curvy tulip skirts for SuperPear in expensive knit fabrics that shimmer while you shake' n' move.

More success stories of curvy/sexy! (Above right and right) Black vinyl jacket, size 4X from Barb's Large and Lovely, black vinyl skirt, size 5X from Love Your Peaches. Black lace-up halter top, 3X, from Barb's Large and Lovely. Cleacia Foster is the lovely model. Photo credit: Skip Orlando.

Curves, and more curves! Tara Weber wears an eye-catching outfit —a beaded strapless halter top with long velvet stretch tube skirt. Strappy shoes complete this dressy and elegantly sexy outfit! Size 14/16. Photo credit: James E. Weber, III.

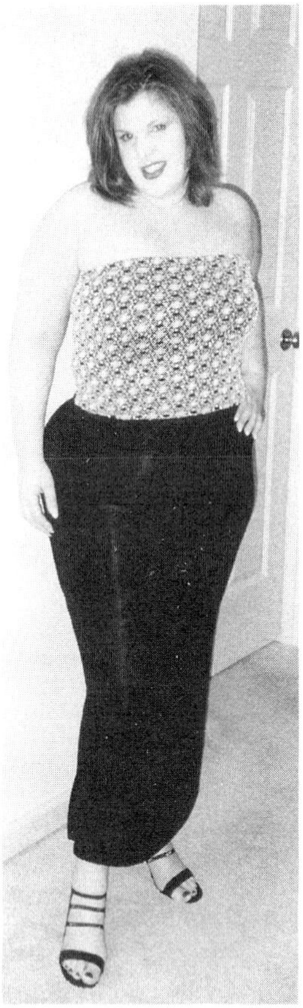

Nothing like a unitard for curvy stretch and comfort! Cathy Bryant poses for us. Navy blue unitard, 90% cotton, 10% spandex, from Lane Bryant. (below) Cathy luxuriates on a white New Zealand wool "bearskin" rug wearing her crushed velvet purple slipdress, 100% polyester. Photo credit on both: Linda Kanzinger.

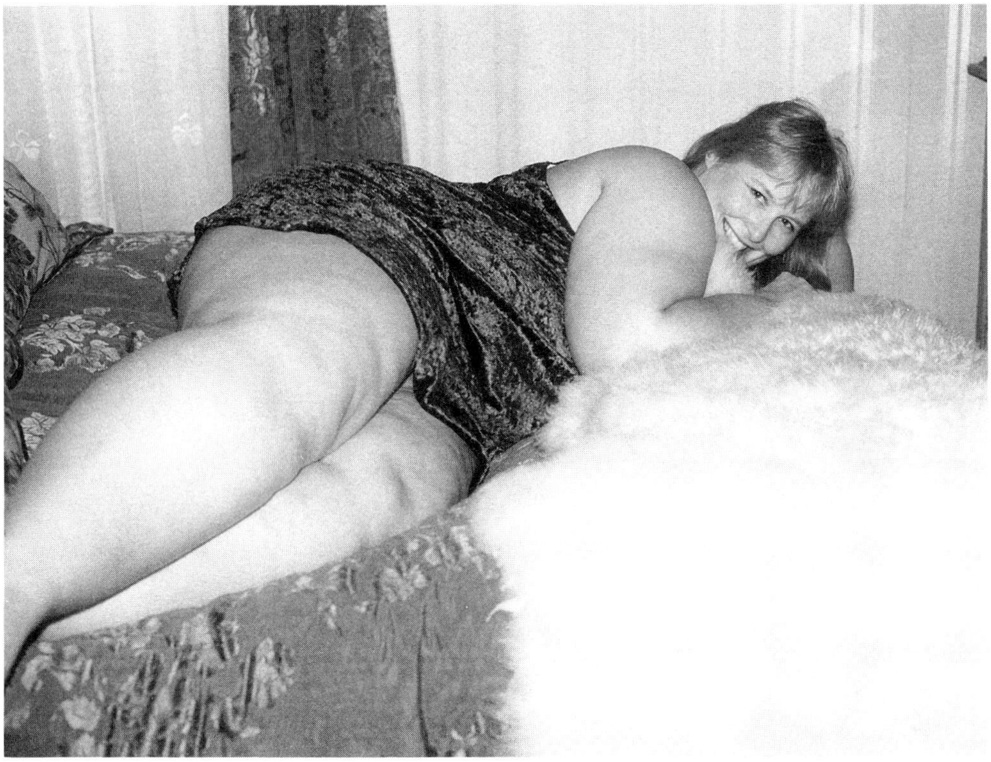

(above) The lovely Cleacia Foster models a powder blue brassiere (24/26W) and panties (28W) with white boa. Photo credit: Skip Orlando.

(above)The stunning Ashley Taylor Clayton wearing a black stretch catsuit, 3X, from Barb's Large and Lovely. Photo credit: Satu.

(above) "Bellie Tag"- Kim Caldwell. Rubber stamped images of goddess women from Her Rubber, stamped lettering, on a tag. Paint, ribbon, edged with gold pen. ©1999 Kim Caldwell. Photo credit: Linda Kanzinger.

WHO SAYS FAT WOMEN CAN'T BE SEXY!

SIZE-POSITIVE STYLE: SOFT/FEMININE

SOFT/FEMININE is a traditional style. Underlying all those bows and frills and lacy things is a statement about women that has its' roots in history. Thus, **Soft/Feminine** doesn't often follow fashion trends, but prefers a traditionally feminine look. She likes the Victorian look: lots of bows and lace. **Soft/Feminine** is also a highly romantic personality. This style emphasizes looking soft, sweet, always nonthreatening, and even shy. She will wear a soft full skirt that shows her legs when she crosses them, rather than the direct sexy look of a very short skirt.

Soft/Feminine is a familiar look. Women who feel innately feminine in the traditional sense will create a sweet and friendly look with soft feminine-looking fabrics which drape. The look is young, also Victorian. She prefers to wear a skirt to pants, and chooses dresses as a mainstay of her wardrobe. White and pink are two favorite colors. Fabrics are draping and soft. Hair and make-up is natural looking; while jewelry is delicate, inconspicuous, and vintage (ie often bought at estate sales). She will buy something because of its' unique look, rather than matching it up with what she already owns, so shopping for clothes is more haphazard than structured. Also, because of the preponderance of light colors, **Soft/Feminine** usually has many more summer clothes than winter clothes.

Color, clothing details, and fabrics include:

Soft and fragile fabrics such as silk
Soft patterns in fabrics
Lots of floral prints
Flowing lines
Pastel colors, light pinks and blues
Ruffles, lace, and ribbons
Princess lines
Interesting detail lines
Bows: on shoes, on socks, on necklines

(Right) F. Tara Weber exudes the Soft/Feminine look in a pink and white print skirt (with matching tie) over which she is wearing a white lacy sweater. Size 14/16. Photo credit: Kelvin Braxton.

(above right) Kelly Ryan modeling a 3-piece ivory-colored lingerie set. Camisole and tap pants, nylon/poly blend; size LT. Robe, 100% polyester, size 2X. Photo credit: Photos by Beth, Mpls, MN.

(above) Beautifully elegant and most feminine—a black sleeveless lacy formal dress, size 4X, by La Reina Boutique, Inc. Black lace over black cotton/rayon blend fabric which criss-crosses in the back. According to the model, Cleacia Foster " it is absolutely the prettiest dress I own.They have the most feminine, romantic clothes that I know of in large sizes." Photo credit: Skip Orlando.

(left) Ashley Taylor Clayton is the star in this mauve catsuit, 100% silk matte stretch lace, part of a pant suit trimmed with Venice lace. Size 3X, from Barb's Large and Lovely. Photo credit: Satu.

and clothing choices include:

Preference for skirts and dresses with flowing lines (A-line, princess line)
Lace underskirts peeking out from full skirts
Gathered skirts in soft cottons and rayons
Blouses with full sleeves, such as peasant or poet blouses
Blouses with ruffles around the neck or along seam lines
Victorian blouses
Draped shirt, pants, with sash tie
Below knee length skirts and dresses
Suits in pastel colors
Full skirts edged with lace or completely of lace
Jumpsuit or pantsuit in a light-colored rayon fabric
Shawls and scarves
Antique jewelry

✓Accent Plus-Size: Renoir looks especially good in **Soft/Feminine** style, as her body shape has the same flowing lines. Venus, with her name sake, the Goddess of Love, is also romantically inclined, and enjoys **Soft/Feminine** style.

✓Accent SuperSize: Since many large women's bodies are soft and feminine, such as SuperPear and Juno, with shapely curves, **Soft/Feminine** is a complimentary style to their body shape. If their personality matches, it works!

✓Subcategories: Western/Prairie

WESTERN/PRAIRIE is a style using a mixture of the Western look, with lots of denim with silver jewelry, and lots of lace such as edging on blouses, flounced skirts, and petticoats. It is definitely a feminine look, spiced with Western appeal.

(clockwise from left)
The impact of pale color is revealed in this flowered pale yellow straw hat worn by Ronda Gregoire (one size). Photo credit: Cindy Butterfield @Dynamic Photography.

(upper right) I dream of being a model....and now I am! muses Tara Weber relaxing in a wine-colored evening dress by La Reina Boutique, Inc. Photo credit: Kelvin Braxton.

(right) Teresa Marie Metcalfe-Johnson in full flower, will be the belle of the ball after she finishes brushing her long curly red hair.... wearing this green velvet slip dress covered with an overdress of burnt-out velvet. A full length babydoll style, size 22. Photo credit: Nancy Metcalfe.

SIZE-POSITIVE STYLE: ARTISTIC/MULTIETHNIC

ARTISTIC/MULTIETHNIC puts together her outfits creatively. She draws from various ethnic groups for ideas in fabrics as well as clothing design. She thinks palette: color, texture, form. The body is the form, the clothing is the vehicle for color and texture, focal point, detail lines, and the entire composition is played with until the desired effect is achieved. Sometimes there are surprises. A scarf changes the entire outfit, so the shoes are then changed, and finally the wine-colored rayon pants complete the outfit!

Artistic/Multiethnic takes from several other styles, but combines them in different ways. And, in truth, **Artistic/Multiethnic** are two branches of the same tree. **Artistic** is the less structured, more randomly creative. **Multiethnic** is a more pull-together look and is often a "statement piece" of pride in ones' heritage.

At first glance, **Artistic/Multiethnic** may appear to duplicate the look of **Dramatic/Headturning**, but they are somewhat different in attitude, personality type, and clothing outfits. **Artistic/Multiethnic** likes to use lots of layers, shops in thrift shops, is a non-conformist, and doesn't care what anyone thinks about her style. Dramatic does care! **Artistic/Multiethnic** also likes to lean into **Soft/Feminine's** closet and borrows a number of items, the lace, the soft " pretties".

Artistic/Multiethnic is a popular style among certain college-age woman, especially progressive types. A lot of attention is also paid to accessories: dangling earrings, silk scarves, ballerina or Chinese cloth shoes, and unusual vintage jewelry. **Artistic/Multiethnic** is also quite interested in historical pieces, and looks in thrift shops just as an archeologist looks for hidden treasures.

Artistic/Multiethnic likes textured fabrics, fabrics with sheen and grain, fabrics that make a statement. She likes clothing styles that "talk", that have an impression, and make an impression. When shopping, she may just go on intuition, and then grab certain things that speak to her. There is no logical stance to either her shopping trips, or in creating outfits. They happen on impulse, but over time, **Artistic/Multiethnic** creates her own specific style, her own creative look.

(above)Gleaming gold jumps out in this bold blue and gold African print two-piece outfit worn by Elsie Bryant. Headwrap completes the outfit. Friend Kim Caldwell accompanies. (below) African fold and dye fabric from Nairobi is fashioned into a favorite two-piece outfit of blue, purple, and white. Tunic-style top with drawstring pants. Size XXL. Modeled by the author at the Juanita Donaldson home. Photo credit: Juanita Donaldson.

(Above) Myra Turley hamming it up with a rose in her mouth! She's wearing a pair of teal colored crinkle rayon overalls with bib with handpainted designs from Peggy Lutz Designs. Size XXL. With off-white cotton shirt, size 3L, straw hat. (Below) Blue-tie-dye rayon jumper from Making It Big, with white T-shirt, both size 4. Photo credit on both: Linda Kanzinger.

The **Artistic/Multiethnic** look is one that fits some BBW women's personality quite well.

Fabrics colors and design lines include:

Handpainted fabrics
Handpainted silk scarves
Combinations of bright colors as a painting
Jewel tone colors: purples, mauves, turquoise, emerald green
Ikat weave fabrics, batiks, tie-dye
100% natural fiber fabrics: cottons, rayons, silks
Flowing loose lines, oversize silhouette

Artistic likes:

The layered look
Vintage or thrift shop clothing
Lots of accessories
Unique interesting fabrics
Oversize clothing, loose lines
Very long skirts
Miniskirts
Unusual color combinations
A slightly unkempt look
"The Black Look"
Antique and unusual jewelry
Platform shoes

while **Multiethnic** prefers:

Handpainted fabrics
Handpainted silk scarves
Combinations of bright colors as a painting
Jewel tone colors: purples, mauves, turquoise, emerald green
Ikat weave fabrics, batiks, tie-dye
100% natural fiber fabrics: cottons, rayons, silks
Flowing lines, oversize silhouette
Handmade jewelry of beads or clay

Outfits for both include:

Gauze skirts and blouses
Rayon blouses with lace
Long denim skirts and dresses
Dresses with panels and overskirts
Leather miniskirts
Ecru or black cotton crochet vests
Cotton tier skirts , "broomstick" skirts
Draped cotton or rayon pants
Handpainted and dyed clothes

✓**Accent Plus-Size:** Tall Reubenesque women can look in the men's section of thrift shops and find interesting jackets, vests, sweaters, and sometimes pants, of an arty style. Small ethnic specialty shops also offer a wide array of artistic interesting looking scarves and jewelry.

✓**Accent SuperSize:** SuperReubenesque women also can discover some "finds" in the men's section of clothing stores and thrift shops, as well as interesting accessories in small ethnic specialty shops as well as in antique stores.

✓**Subcategories: The Layered Look, Vintage, The Leather Look**

(above) "Bodacious Babe", ie, the author, wearing beaded cherry red sweater and purple tam. 55% ramie, 45% cotton, size 2X. Glossy black bugle beads are embroidered on the front in swirled designs. (below right) Ashley Taylor Clayton is seductively sensual in her flower print rayon scarf with silver bangles. Photo credit: Satu.

THE LAYERED LOOK is often used by **Artistic** as it fits her spontaneous mood so well!

VINTAGE is a pure style: it takes **Artistics** favorites, just making sure they are all "vintage", to pull off this co-ordinated look.

THE LEATHER LOOK is also a pure style, with leather as the centerpiece. Leather pants with a matching leather halter top and perhaps a fringed vest, complete with boots, makes the outfit.

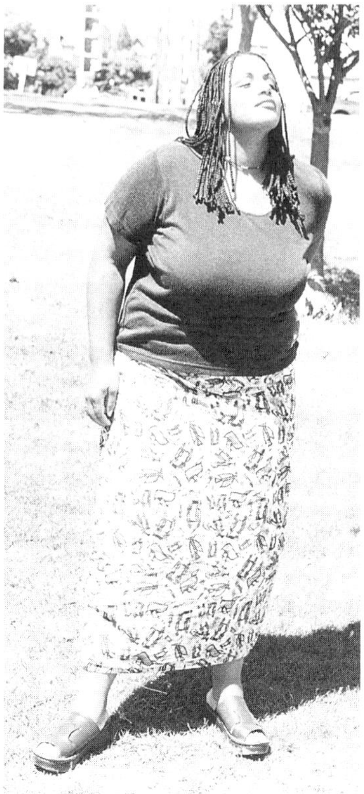

(left) Tesia Johnson enjoying the sunshine in a long African print wrap. 100% cotton, size 26W. She's also wearing a brown 50/50 polycotton T-shirt, size 26W, with brown leather mules. Photo credit: Hansi.

(above) Green and gold African print dress with gold embroidery, front-pleated, gold with red edging, also with black-edged tapered hem, and inner drawstring belt. Caftan style. With headwrap of same print material. From The African Village "One Size Fits Most". This elegant ethnic style dress is a pleasure to behold, and a treasure to wear. Andrea Hall does the honors on this one! Photo credit: Linda Kanzinger.

SIZE-POSITIVE STYLE: CLASSIC/CAREER

Just a few soft curves and a cherubic expression for Andrea Hall modeling her tencel (acetate/spandex) olive green button-down long sleeved shirt, size 26/28W, with black tencel long pants, size 22/24W. Photo credit: Linda Kanzinger.

Gabby Sparapani models a white shirt, cotton jacket, beaded vest, and stirrup pants.

CLASSIC/CAREER is a well-known and popular style. Since women joined the work force, career wear has expanded to make up a great part of women's fashion. In fact, in the plus and supersizes, career wear predominates. One reason is that manufacturers found it easy to make the transition up to larger sizes without having to "risk their shirt" on unknown styles. This included a majority of plus-size women with office careers who wear suits and traditional separates.Therefore, most retail stores are jam packed with this style of clothing.

Classic/Career has also been covered in detail by many fashion writers, so I feel it is better known to most readers than other styles. The basic look includes tailored suits, silk or rayon blouses, low pumps, subdued jewelry—in all a fairly traditional look. The choice of luxurious fabrics can extend the look from a tailored impression to a feminine, yet still very official look.

Classic/Career is epitomized by control, organized, and restrained taste. Tailored clothes, designer clothes, and status symbol accessories all appeal to her. She is not open to much change in her wardrobe, however, she does attend to fashion changes and will update her wardrobe with accessory items (scarves, shoes, handbag, hats, belts, etc).

Sometimes the straight-lined look of the **Classic/Career** is at odds with the rounded Reubenesque body, so that in plus and supersize clothing, the design lines are more flowing than in the average-sized classic look.

Colors, fabrics, and style lines include:

Tailored, fitted garments
Expensive, good quality fabrics, such as silk and wool
Gabardine, tweed, cotton and cotton blends, rayons
Neutral colors (black, brown, cream, grey)
Straight lines to slightly relaxed fit

(above) Ms Cheryl Anderson as she returns from a long day's work! She's classy in her red fleece coat, XXL, her black and white striped rayon slacks, 20W, and her black canvas briefcase. Photo credit: John L. Smith. (left) Liza Joy looks classically elegant in her bright pink silk jacket, size 16W, with short black viscose rayon skirt, 16W, and stretchy silk black top. Size 16W. Photo credit: Yan Dollar.

and clothing selection includes:

Tailored suits in dark colors
Cotton, rayon, and natural silk fitted blazers
Ensemble dressing (coordinated blazer, blouse, skirt)
Tailored pants suit (blazer and dress pants)
Tailored dress slacks in quality fabrics
Silk blouses
Slightly A-line polished cotton and gabardine skirts
Straight skirts
Fluid, unfitted jacket
Soft draping skirt
Layered look
Easy separates (not so tightly coordinated)
Tailored jumpsuit
Fluid lines with more body exposure
Textured knits
Evening gown with draped lines
Silk pants
Knit tops
Rayon walking shorts
Hosiery is usually dark and coordinated with low-heeled shoes

✓Accent Plus-Size: Classic/Career is popular with the Apple and Box or Rectangular body shapes due to the straight lines of both. The rectangular shapes of tailored blazers and tailored skirts or pants harmonize with the straight-line body shapes of the Apple and the Box.

✓Accent SuperSize: SuperReubenesque's shape works best with the straight lines of **Classic/Career**, although Supersize Scallop often successfully wears these clothes as well.

✓Subcategories: Menswear, Elite/Power Dressing, Frenchstyle/European

MENSWEAR depends on man-tailored blazers as well as traditional career fabrics such as tweeds.

ELITE/POWER DRESSING is upscale fashion, with expensive-looking well-tailored suits meant to impress, and show power.

FRENCHSTYLE/EUROPEAN is best described by the types of clothing offered by companies such as Ulla Popken (see appendix).

ALTERNATIVE AND SUBORDINATE STYLES STYLES I: A SUBCULTURE OF STYLES

Another way to look at styles is to divide them into **MAINSTREAM STYLES,** which have been discussed above, and **ALTERNATIVE STYLES,** of which there are plenty.

The first selection are subcategories of the major styles:

From **Confident:**
- **The Cotton Look**
- **The Denim Look**
- **Student/Thrift Store**

From **Romantic:**
- **Western/Prairie**
- **Vintage**

From **Dramatic:**
- **Leather/Biker**
- **Punk**

From **Artistic:**
- **The Layered Look**
- **Vintage**
- **The Black Look**
- **Bohemian/Hippie**
- **Avant-Guarde/Hip**

From **Classic:**
- **Menswear**
- **Frenchstyle/European**
- **Elite/Power Dressing**

(upper right) Don't let those eyes distract from an all out showstopper of a shirt! Blue cowboy shirt, with silver bolero tie reveals the Western look! Poly/cotton blend, modeled by Stella Kuperberg. Photo credit: Kevin Kuperberg.(lower right) Carol L. Gautney,II wearing cowhide leather motorcycle jacket with 100% polyester lining. Men's size 46, vented for airflow.

Avant-Guarde/Hip: the most faddish of these styles, Avant-Guarde is always on the cutting edge of fashion.

Bohemian/Hippie: Bright colors, ethnic styles and fabrics, handpainted and dyed fabrics are the staple for the hippie or bohemian look. Clothing is flowing, fabrics are usually 100% natural fiber. Handmade jewelry completes the look.

Elite/Power Dressing: While probably still a minor style for fat women, there are a small percentage of curvaceous women in fast-track careers who power dress, wearing expensive clothing of name designers in order to impart a sense of superior status and elitism. Other people who wear this type of expensive clothing would include the wealthy, and royalty.

Leather/Biker: Leather jackets and pants, leather miniskirts or teddies, chains, studded collars or bracelets, and bandeaux or crop tops that show lots of cleavage.

Menswear, popular in the early 80's, merely traded off some of men's dress clothing into women's clothing. Instead of wearing a skirt with a blazer, you wear a pair of tailored trousers in greys and tweeds. Often shoes are sturdy, leather, tied, formidable and totally comfortable.

Western/Prairie: an offshoot of the Romantic look, Western/Prairie style includes gathered skirts of cotton or denim with flounces and an underskirt of lace, prairie style or poet's blouses.

Vintage: 40's and 50's style dresses, velveteen smoking jackets, linen and rayon pants and blazers, fine 100% cotton shirts, antique jewelry, shoes, hosiery, scarves.

(upper right) Carol L. Gautney II, wearing a long-sleeved form-fitting ankle length blue dress of 90% polyester/ 10% spandex fabric. Medium size. With sterling silver glue gem Renaissance necklace. Size 20/22W. (lower right) Cleacia Foster in her "biker chick" outfit: custom made leather halter, and size 22/24W leggings. Maybe a studded necklace, too! Photo credit: Skip Orlando.

SIZE-POSITIVE STYLE: MOTIFS

This second selection are styles that I have named or grouped. Some of these styles are included above.

Anti-Authority: This includes goths, cyberpunks, and skaters, and many of the fads listed in the Alternative and Subcultural Styles in the next section. Usually worn by the young, the clothing sends the message of a clear distinction between the wearer and mainstream society.

Fat women are already treated as if they are clearly "outside"of mainstream society, so there might be a question as to why young full-bodied women would want to emphasize their social differentness. I think young phat women should have the same choices as other young women, to rebel, to dress as their peers dress, to express their individuality through clothing.

(above left) Kelly Ryan in a black sleeveless knit dress, rib knit. Knit fabric flows over the curves of a voluptuous woman. 100% cotton, 2X, from Love Your Peaches. (left) Kelly Ryan wears a black princess style, knee-length dress of polyester velour, size 18/20W. The flair of this style as well as the texture of the fabric creates visual delight!

The Black Look: Is a fat woman wearing black in the winter wearing "camouflage clothing", or is a fat woman wearing black simply wearing black? We as Reubenesque women have the right to claim wearing black as "the black look", not as the "trying to slenderize look" or the "cover me up look". Black is a sexy color. It is also utilitarian, especially for city wear. It provides a backdrop for jewelry or a "statement piece" such as a fabric painted scarf.

Clothes to See and Be Seen In: These are the kinds of clothes that, when you see them on someone else, you rush up to them and ask them "what kind of fabric is that? Where did you get that beautiful dress?" And, when you wear them, other people do that to you! Similar to **Dramatic/Headturning,** these are clothes you wear when you want heads to turn! Beautiful fabrics, bold handpainted dresses, and glittery goddess dresses are some of the many types of clothes in this category.

The Cotton Look: 100% roomy cotton tops, shirts, big shirts, gauzy layered jumpers, the Cotton Look is a freshfaced, natural, scrubbed clean look. Usually in whites or off-whites, with loose lines, clothing is comfortable and breathable, which is especially nice for the larger phat woman.

The Denim Look: Denim has moved beyond a Western look to include jumpers, big shirts, gathered skirts, as well as jeans, jean shorts, skorts, rompers, culottes, etc. Colors include white, black, as well as traditional blue. There is the stone-washed look and other surface treatments as well. The Denim Look is a natural, durable, practical look, with style.

Fashion to Fad: This look is seen more often on the younger set, but is also worn by all ages in fashion centers of the country and in progressive big cities. It includes clothing such as: mini skirts with a big oversize sweater, print leggings, crop pants, Lycra bicycle and work out shorts, gauzy culottes, and rayon and silk blouses, shirts and big shirts.

Highlight/Camouflage Style: These work in tandem. You highlight one part of the body, conceal or camouflage another, such as wearing a sleeveless low-cut crop top with a pair of long cotton gauze wrap pants with slits.

"FAT WOMEN HAVE THE RIGHT TO WEAR BLACK, JUST LIKE EVERYONE ELSE, RATHER THAN HAVING IMPOSED ON US ONLY ONE MEANING— TO SLENDERIZE OUR FIGURE. WE HAVE THE RIGHT TO EXPRESS WHAT WEARING BLACK MEANS TO US,

Kelly Ryan models a black sequin, scoop neck, form-fitting dress. Polyester, with silk lining. Size 20WP. Photo credit: Photos by Beth, Mpls, MN.

AND NOT RESIDE IN THE JAIL OF 'ONLY ONE MEANING'."

(left) Refreshing whites, a blend of separates with remarkable clarity, almost as tangible as the crisp salt air! 100% cotton gauze jacket, pants and tank top, size 26/28W. Stacey Richardson is the casual conspirator to this relaxing scene.

I-Must-talk-To-You Style: Compliments of Shilo George, of Portland, OR, these are clothes that are so compelling and put together in such an original manner that others are drawn to you and thus, must talk to you!

The Layered Look: with long, draping roomy clothing made from silk, rayon, and lightweight cottons. Especially nice for the larger plus size and supersize woman, as it allows breathability and comfort. Various combinations include tapered pants with a loose top and duster coat; top and coat can have sleeves or be sleeveless; gathered or pleated skirt with tunic styled top, with side slits in both skirt and top are several examples of this style.

Laborer/Working: Healthy women working in the trades are going to need common-sense clothes. There's a practical aspect to this with jobs requiring lifting, or standing on cement floors in factories. Men's corduroy and flannel shirts, jeans, longsleeved loose knit sweaters— lots of big women wear "plain clothes". Also look for uniforms in men's stores that are used in carpentry and other trades.

(lower right) F. Tara Weber sports a fresh nautical look with navy blue clamdiggers, red top, white jacket, red and white head scarf. Size 14/16.Photo credit: James E. Weber III.

(lower left) Gabby Sparapani poses in a casual outfit of cut-off jeans, size 24(44) with 100% cotton sweatshirt.

Make Fat Visible " Let It Swing" Style: You've got fat, flaunt it! Or at least show it. Knit tops, knit stirrup pants reveal soft bodies and put some umph in your step. Since the body of a fat women is itself a sculpture, with many folds and layers, when you move, that fat dances and swings. Fabrics such as tencel and ribbed knits move and sway when you move.

Revealing Style: Crop tops to expose bare midriffs, short shorts to reveal big calves and thighs, sleeveless styles, low-cut styles. In a bigger body you might want sometimes to reveal only arms, or legs, not always both at the same time. Wrap pants which have open side slits. Side and back slits in skirts.

Summer Supersize Style: Bright colors, especially reds, oranges, yellows, summer is not a time to hide! Wear layers of breezy gauzy fabrics, cotton gauze, lightweight silks, see-through textured cottons in whites, light colors. Add big loppy straw summertime hats to keep cool, plus canvas or straw sandals. Wear the "double sleeveless look" : a cotton sleeveless top over which you wear a long sleeveless tunic-styled vest or duster coat. Sleeveless jumpers with sleeveless T's underneath are also fun!

SIZE-NEGATIVE STYLES: STYLES TO AVOID

Hopefully, very few zoftig women still dress this way. However, if you are one of them, this book is chock full of more exciting choices!

Covering: Historically, this style has been worn by many supersize women as well as plus-size women, and for many good reasons, primarily, the size discriminatory society which is so verbally abusive to both, but especially to supersize women.

Poor Look/SDS This style (SDS stands for Self-Defeating Style) is worn by women of low economic status who also have low self-esteem. The basic philosophy is "I'm fat, so it doesn't matter anyway."

The Over-and-Over Style: You see it over and over, the empire styled dress with the sleeves to the elbow, never above. The hemline is always right above the ankle. It's made in wool and corduroy and heavy cotton in the winter, and in lighter fabrics for the summer. It supposedly is so popular because it fits so many body shapes. The problem is, it looks like **Covering Style.** It is especially prevalent in supersizes.

Wash N Wear: I call it "no iron, no style" — but— many women swear by polyester and acetate separates. In general, it is a more conservative casual style found in smaller, rural communities.

(left) In a dramatic flare, Mel Roberts tries to spook us in her Goth look of black rayon cloak, size 28/30W, with ballerina slippers, and bright red lipstick!

FADS AND FAT: ALTERNATIVE AND SUBCULTURE STYLES: 2

The following styles, as well as fads, are from a variety of subcultures and street culture. In thinking about them for plus and supersize women, I found myself thinking about the relationship between having what the mainstream perceives as a low-status, socially disapproved body, and wearing clothes that in themselves communicate social distrust, rebellion, anti-fashion, youth, and an anti-mainstream culture. There is an interesting juxtaposition between the point of many of these alternative styles: rebellion against the mainstream, and the **SOCIALLY UNSANCTIONED BODY OF THE FAT WOMAN.**

How many fat women are going to be drawn, say, to the antisocial look of Punk, with spiked green and orange hair, studded leather jackets and pants, body piercing, and the use of oversized safety pins? Are Reubenesque young women going to adopt the Skaters style — extra-large, brightly patterned long oversized shorts, T-shirts with bright colors and patterns, its' "studied scruffiness"? Or what about Goth? Is a curvaceous young woman going to look good wearing black fishnet stockings, black leather, dyed black hair, high stiletto heels, tightly laced corsets, above the elbow black leather gloves, white pancake makeup, blood-red, or blackberry, lipstick, and silver jewelry with religious or occult themes?

As mentioned in Chapter I, many fashion books emphasized that the large women needed to be ""impeccably dressed", held to a higher standard because of her socially unsanctioned body. Now, a number of these subcultural styles could quite accurately be described as pushing the edge. How does the phat women adapt some of these more "outrageous" styles on an already socially disapproved body?

I do not feel we need to "prove " to a size discriminatory country that we are OK by always appearing in public "impeccably dressed". To do so is to oppose the choices that I feel big women should also have, especially when young, when fads in clothing are important identity statements. We, as bodacious zoftig women, should never be held to a "higher standard" because of the prejudice of others!

"The juxtaposition of alternative styles with the already "alternative" fat body is an interesting one.

I was at a social event with a number of fat people who were sloppily dressed. Or dressed down. Or dressed poor.

Some of them could have fit into the category of "grunge". But our society, in dismissing fat people in any way serious, probably couldn't conceive of a fat person intentionally wearing "grunge".

Remember, young people are killing themselves rather than facing the ridicule of their high school peers teasing them for being fat."

(left) "Fairy" by Dimitri Kare. 2.5"x3" Pen and ink/computer drawing. First commissioned for a rubber stamp design. © Dimitri Kare.

I want these cutting edge or faddish styles to be seen as "spices". I also want to validate the differences in fashion for young women of dimension and middle aged and older women. Most of the fads, after all, are for the young (and the young at heart!)

Many young people in their late teens and 20's follow **Alternative Style,** but gradually fade into **Mainstream Style** when they need to work full-time. As well, many styles start out in a segment of an Alternative culture and are eventually picked up by the mainstream fashion industry. Of course, some of the styles are so " far out" that they don't make it any farther than the catwalk or the pages of a trendy fashion magazine!

I refer you to the books *StreetStyle* by Ted Polhemus, and *Surfers Soulies Skinheads and Skaters: Subcultural Style from the Fourties to the Nineties* by Amy de la Haye and Cathie Dingwall, for definitions of the following, as well as many photographic examples.

Afrocentric
B-Boy
Beatnik (Beats)
Cyberpunk
Eco
Fetish (Pervs)
Funk
Gay Style
Glam
Goth
Greasers
Grunge
Head-banger
Hippie (Hippy)
Hipsters
Indie
Mod
New Age (Travellers)
New Romantics
Preppy
Psychedelic
Rockabilly
Punk
Rasta (Rastafarian)
Raves
Rocker
Skater
Surfer
Zoot Suiter

STYLES AND ARCHETYPES

All of these styles express various archetypes, which are original forms or symbols of a variety of feelings, concepts, and personality traits. Styles can express women's different selves. That's why it is important to me that women of dimension have the same choices in fashion that other women have. There is something, unfortunately, that limits our choice. It is how we are still perceived.

ARCHETYPAL IMAGES OF FAT WOMEN

There are many primary or original images of fat women. Think of all the words I have used in this book to describe us: Goddess, big, fat, woman of dimension, phat, Reubenesque, curvaceous, bodacious, healthy, woman of substance, full-figured, zoftig, mid-size, plus-size, supersize, abundant, thick, BBW. Then there are the many negative images and associations of fat women. I won't list them all here— we are familiar with them. However, they permeate the fashion world and how clothing designers perceive us, our bodies, and thus the types of clothing they design for us.

While at an
upscale department store's fashion show several
springtimes ago,
I checked out
the swimwear.
90 % of the styles were either of black fabric,
or had black in the fabric.
There were no bikinis,
and no 2-piece suits except for one that
completely covered the body. Whether conscious
or not,
the message sent was that a fat woman wasn't a
sexy woman,
and didn't "deserve"
bright colors
or a variety of styles.

We have to consistently and continually fight how others see a big female body. Unfortunately, there are unconscious images attached to the goddess form. People may not be aware that they perceive a large woman as motherly, asexual, and nurturing, simply because her body is ample. In the previous discussion about "impeccably dressed" the unspoken perception is that a full-figured woman is sloppy or slovenly just by virtue of her size.

Unfortunately, even now, a preponderance of plus sized clothing in the stores are fairly mainstream to conservative. Supersize women have few choices in going to stores, and rely upon trunk shows attached to size-acceptance conventions and activities, as well as using professional seamstresses. As well, young women express a need for more youthful styles and stylish fashions for going out to clubs. Supersize women want clothes that are "fun" as well, that express humor and lightness, not so serious or staid.

SIZE-POSITIVE ARCHETYPES OF FAT WOMEN

One of the underpinnings of this book is to present new visual messages of fat women—as strong individualized people. A size-positive view of style presents our womanly bodies, with curves, weight, flesh, and substance, as attractive rather than in a negative light. These new archetypes can include the following:

- **the sexy fat woman**
- **the strong fat woman**
- **the active limber and flexible fat woman**
- **the romantic dreamily desirable fat woman**

Once you realize you are not limited to these dated size-negative archetypes, but instead, can pick and choose from a whole variety of styles, then the negative archetypes surrounding fat women dissipate.

WE CAN DENY 2ND CLASS CITIZENSHIP WITH SIZE-POSITIVE STYLE!

APPENDIX OF CONTRIBUTORS

ARTISTS

Dimitri Kare: is a native of Russia, currently living in the US. He was trained in Moscow, Rome and Philadelphia and participated in shows and sold his work to art collectors in the U.S. and Europe. Dimitri's paintings were featured twice in BBW Magazine. For more art samples and information see: http://members.aol.com/dmitrikare E-mail: DmitriKare@aol.com or write to: Dimitri Kare, 7 Tennyson Drive, Plainsboro, NJ 08536 Tel: (609)275-6491

Lis Gede: Selfmade painter, cartoonist, illustrator, writer and translator. Lives and works in Copenhagen, Denmark. Email: gede @ image.dk.Website: http://members.aol.com/jeffryw/

T'Rina Headlee: 31, an artist and writer from Boise Idaho who is using her art and words to explore and show people the beauty of large women. http://www.geocities.com/msxxl

Kim Caldwell : I am a rubber stamp artist, also make jewelry, handmade paper and journals.

MODELS

Cheryl Anderson: 49, I love to do physical things, hiking and biking, snowshoeing. I've struggled with size all my life, but at this time I am coming to accept it and am pleased with who I am.

Bella: 34, 5'2", Professional Model for fun; Engineer to pay the bills; Artist for my spirituality, ie, dancer, painter, poet, seamstress; love music, the ocean, the beach, dolphins. My passion is life. Email: hi2bella@mail.com.

Cathy Bryant: 33, Oregon, love to have fun. Into scuba diving and travel. I am a first time model and loved working with Linda. Email: Summer@uswest.net.

Elsie Bryant: Educator at George Meany College; labor union historian and performer.

Enid D. Caccavelli: 36, animal lover, horror fan, avid collector of Precious Moments and Charming Tails figurines, full-time mom with big dreams. Would love to model professionally if anyone is interested. You can contact me at LuvPMs777@aol.com.

Kim Caldwell : 43, special needs educator, labor union activist. Animal lover. Email: cluwor@aol.com

Jeri Carmichael: 45, programmer/analyst, people lover, cat lover, cross-stitcher, traveler. jericarmichael@msn.com.

Andrea E. Cipala: 50, world-travelled, loves to dance, sings from the depth of her soul, lives life with joie de vivre and a smattering of la vida loca to add color to life's journey.

Ashley Taylor Clayton: professional plussize model and actress who has appeared in BBW, Bella, on the cover of Radiance magazine, also film, TV, commercials, and a music video. Email: amber@emailfyi.com. Websites: http://lovingyoularge.com/lobby/ashley.htm; http://www.proaxis.com/~sherlockfam/bbw4.html.

Emanon: professional model, shopper, make-up artist, poetry writer and adventurer. 888-477-8025. Dress 14/16 Height: 5'11" Bust 42D, Waist 38, Hips 46, Shoes 10/11. P.O. Box 43103 Detroit, MI 48243

Cleacia Foster: Cleacia Foster Freelance Photographer and former plus size model. http://www.catay.com/cleacia/. Specializing in BBW photography.

Carol Gautney, II 24, writer, artist, treasure hunter, and aspiring professional wrestler. Contact address: Baby Carol, P.O. Box 831, San Luis, CO 81152.

Nancy Goddess: Goddesses Parties for Big Beautiful Women and Big Men and their Admirers. Weekly parties. Website: Http://hometown.aol.com/GoddessInc/index.html. Phone: 718-456-9119. Email: GoddessInc@aol.com.

Ronda Gregoire: I'm 29, a fulltime student, I'm a big family person so anything with my family (husband and one son) is what I love (like picnics, hiking, small vacations, etc.)

Andrea Hall: I am currently attending college part-time and working full-time. I welcome all positive responses and comments. BTRUE2YOSELF@AOL.com.

Teresa Marie Metcalfe-Johnson: Accomplished full-figured model, actress, vocalist and poet. Always searching for new opportunities. Can be reached at (email) theedivatoo@cs.com.Website forthcoming.

Tesia Johnson: Website: http://plusmodels.com/Tesia/. Is currently represented by: Cast Images Talent Agency, 717 20th St. #250, Sacramento, CA 95814. (916)444-9655. Please contact Chondra Bourne for booking information.
Liza Joy: P.O. Box 66150 1106 Wilson Ave. Toronto Ont. M3M1G7, e-mail lizajoy@globalserve.net, website www.moscownights.org. From Russian descent, as well as adventurer and animal lover.
Linda Kanzinger, 48, owner of The Alcott Press, writer, artist, gardener and homesteader, cat and rabbit lover, adventurer. Email me at: alcottpres@aol.com!
Sharon Klose, 35 years old, retired nurse, now homemaker married to John. They enjoy their cats, the beach at sunset and fine dining. Hobbies include cooking, baking, crossword puzzles and music. Residence St. Petersburg, FL and e-mail address: klose1@tampabay.rr.com.
Jennie Middleton: 21, model, actress, award winning photographer. Can be contacted at 760-743-6130 for any modeling jobs.
Cat Nordling: 32, model although web development is my "real job". Contact address: 66 E. 9th Street # 1916, St Paul, MN 55101. Web: http://www.catay.com/ Email: cat@ catay.com. Interests: art, theater, movies, swimming, self-acceptance and travel.
Stacey Richardson: age 30, size 24-26. Contact: MAGOSTANG@aol.com or 803-318-0624 Interests: plus size clothing and art designing.
Mel Roberts: P.O. Box 36798 Canton, OH 44735.
Kelly Ryan: 31, size 18/20, WarmerInMO@aol.com, plus modeling experience.
Lynne Shaw: 44, Massachusetts, nurse, retired firefighter, owner of Quabbin Healthcare Consulting. www.quabbinhealthcare.com home page. 4-H volunteer, mother to cats, rabbits, and a Chincoteague Pony. Novice writer, persistent gardener, enjoying every moment of life! Email: Lynnie40@aol.com.
Myra Turley: over-the-hill clothes horse, artist, gardener, quilter, dreaming about my next vacation.
Voluptuous Images: Http://www.voluptuous.nu/modeling/ Email: Lynda@voluptuous.nu.
Delores Young: postal worker, labor union activist.

BIBLIOGRAPHY

FASHION BOOKS FOR THE SIZE-POSITIVE WOMEN

Farro, Rita. **LIFE IS NOT A DRESS SIZE:** Rita Farro's Guide to Attitude, Style, and a New You. Radnor, PA: Chilton Books, 1996. 136 pages, $16.95.

Foley, Valerie. **PLUS SIZE MODELING FOR FUN.** 65 pages, $18.00. www.venusimaging.com

Lane Bryant. **THE LANE BRYANT LARGE WOMEN FASHION MATH MAKEOVER:** The Complete Fashion Guide for Women Size 14 and Up.NY: Dell Publishing, 1987. 128 pages.

Marano, Hara Estroff. **STYLE IS NOT A SIZE: LOOKING AND FEELING GREAT IN THE BODY YOU HAVE.** NY: Bantam Books, 1991. 338 pages, $15.00.

Mathis, Carla Mason and Connor, Helen Villa. **THE TRIUMPH OF INDIVIDUAL STYLE:** A Guide to Dressing your body, your beauty, your self. Menlo Park,CA: Timeless Editions, 1993. 183 pages, $24.95.

Nanfeldt, Suzan. **PLUS STYLE:** The Plus Size Guide to Looking Great. NY: Plume/Penguin Books, 1996.325 pages, $19.95.

Roberts, Nancy. **BREAKING ALL THE RULES: FEELING GOOD AND LOOKING GREAT NO MATTER WHAT YOUR SIZE.** NY: Viking Penguin,1985. 220 pages, $17.95

Sullivan, Judy. **SIZE WISE:** A Catalogue of More Than 1000 Resources for Living With Confidence and Comfort at Any Size. NY: Avon Books, 1997. 385 Pages, $12.00 .

Zangrillo, Frances Leto. **FASHION DESIGN FOR THE PLUS-SIZE.** NY: Fairchild Publications, 1990.191 pages.

GENERAL FASHION BOOKS

Cho, Emily and Fisher, Neila. **IT'S YOU: LOOKING TERRIFIC, WHATEVER YOUR TYPE.** NY: Ballantine, 1986.185 pages, $7.95.

Cho, Emily and Grover, Linda. LOOKING TERRIFIC: EXPRESS YOURSELF THROUGH THE LANGUAGE OF CLOTHING. NY: G.P. Putnam's Sons, 1978. 205 pages.

Cho, Emily and Lueders, Hermine. LOOKING, WORKING, LIVING TERRIFIC 24 HOURS A DAY: GET YOUR LIFE IN ORDER WITH PERSONAL STYLE. NY: Putnam's. 1982. 154 pages, $13.95.

De La Haye, Amy, and Dingwall, Cathie. SURFERS SOULIES SKINHEADS AND SKATERS: Subcultural Style from the Fourties to the Nineties. Woodstock, NY: The Overlook Press, 1996.

Fatt, Amelia. CONSERVATIVE CHIC: THE FIVE-STEP PROGRAM FOR DRESSING WITH STYLE. NY: Times Books, 1983.

Feldon, Leah. DRESSING RICH:A GUIDE TO CLASSIC CHIC FOR WOMEN WITH MORE TASTE THAN MONEY. NY: G.P. Putnam's Sons, 1982.

Feldon, Leah. DRESS LIKE A MILLION (ON CONSIDERABLY LESS): A RECESSION-PROOF GUIDE TO STYLE IN THE 1990'S. NY: Villard Books, 1993. 192 pages, $20.00.

Fenner, Anne and Burns, Sandi. DRESS SMART: A GUIDE TO EFFECTIVE PERSONAL PACKAGING. NY: Fairchild Publications, 1988.199 pages.

Hensler, Tracy and Dougherty, Karla. SLEEK CHIC: HEAD-TO-TOE FASHION STRAGETIES FOR FIXING FIGURE FLAWS. NY: Putnam Publishing Group, 1988. Skylight Press, 1987. 175 pages.

Jackson, Carole. COLOR ME BEAUTIFUL: DISCOVER YOUR NATURAL BEAUTY THROUGH THE COLORS THAT MAKE YOU LOOK GREAT AND FEEL FABULOUS. Washington, DC: Acropolis Books, Ltd, 1980.

Kibbe, David. METAMORPHOSIS: DISCOVER YOUR IMAGE IDENTITY. NY: Atheneum, 1987.

Leopold, Allison Kyle & Cloutier, Anne Marie. SHORT CHIC: THE EVERYTHING-YOU-NEED-TO-KNOW FASHION GUIDE FOR EVERY WOMAN UNDER 5'4". NY: Rawson, Wade Publishers, Inc. 1981. 244 pages.

McJimsey, Harriet T. ART AND FASHON IN CLOTHING SELECTION. Ames, IA: Iowa State University Press, 1973.

Nethery, Betty. UNIQUELY YOU. Carol Stream: Tyndale House Pub, 1984.

Parsons, Alyce and Parente, Diane. UNIVERSAL STYLE:DRESS FOR WHO YOU ARE AND WHAT YOU WANT.Ross, CA: Parente and Parsons, 1991. 150 pages.

Pearce, Carol Ann CAREER CHIC: What Every Woman Should Know About Getting Ahead in Style. Putnam Pub. Group, 1990.

Pooser, Doris. ALWAYS IN STYLE: HOW TO MAKE FASHION WORK FOR YOU. Washington, DC: Acropolis Books Ltd, 1985.

Pooser, Doris. SECRETS OF STYLE. Los Altos, CA: Crisp Publications, Inc. 1992. 120 pages.

Robin, Jennifer. CLOTHE YOUR SPIRIT: DRESSING FOR SELF-EXPRESSION. Anaheim, CA: Spirit Press, 1988.

Segerstrom, Jane. STYLE STRATEGY: WINNING THE APPEARANCE GAME. Houston, TX: Triad Press, 1988. 160 pages, $14.95.

Tate, Sharon. INSIDE FASHION DESIGN. NY: Watson-Guptill, Inc. 1994.

Takamura, Zeshu. ROOTS OF STREET STYLE. Toyko, Japan: Graphic-sha Publishing Co. Ltd. 1997. 207 pages, $39.95.

Wallace, Joanne. DRESS WITH STYLE. Old Tappan, NJ: Revell, 1983.

Wallach, Janet. LOOKS THAT WORK: HOW TO MATCH YOUR WARDROBE TO YOUR PROFESSIONAL PROFILE AND CREATE THE IMAGE THAT IS RIGHT FOR YOU. NY: Viking, 1986. 253 pages.

Weiland, Barbara and Wood, Leslie. CLOTHES SENSE. Palmer and Pletsch Associates, 1984.

GODDESS BOOKS

Austen, Hallie Iglehart. **THE HEART OF THE GODDESS: ART, MYTH AND MEDITATIONS OF THE WORLD'S SACRED FEMININE.** Berkeley, CA: Wingbow Press, 1990, 164 pages, $24.95.

Edison, Laurie Toby and Notkin, Debbie Edison. **WOMEN EN LARGE: IMAGES OF FAT NUDES.** Books In Focus, 1994, 119 pages $24.95.

Gadon, Elinor W. **THE ONCE AND FUTURE GODDESS.** SF: Harper and Row, 1989. 432 pages, $29.00.

Gimbutas, Marija. **THE GODDESSES AND GODS OF OLD EUROPE: MYTHS AND CULT IMAGES.** Berkeley and Los Angeles, CA: The University of California Press, 1982. 304 pages.

MAGAZINES

BBW Real Women Real Beauty. for women size 16+. Publisher Lisa Krebs. Editor-in Chief: Sally E Smith. Toll-free 1-877-BBW-STYLE. Website: www.bbwmagazine.com. Aeon Publishing Company, Inc 88 Sunnyside Blvd. Suite 203 Plainview, NY 11803 Yearly subscriptions $14.95 for 6 issues. BBW HAS BEEN AROUND SINCE THE 1970'S. A FEW YEARS AGO IT WAS SOLD, AND HAS RE-EMERGED EVEN STRONGER THAN EVER. LOTS OF FASHION IN THIS MAGAZINE.

Belle The Premier Magazine for Confident full-figured women. 1-800-877-5549 Starlog Group Inc 475 Park Ave South, New York, NY 10016 Yearly subscriptions $12.97 for 4 issues. BELLE IS A BLACK FASHION MAGAZINE FOR ALL BIG WOMEN. IT SHOWS LOTS OF SUPERSIZE CURVY WOMEN AS WELL AS MANY FULL-BODIED PLUS SIZES. NO SMALL SIZES MASQUERADING AS PLUS IN THIS MAGAZINE! LOTS OF FASHIONS.

Dimensions The Magazine for Plus-Size Women and Their Admirers. Editor-in-Chief Conrad Blickenstorfer, VP Operations Ruby Blickenstorfer. PO Box 640, Folsom, CA 95763-0640. Website: http://dimensionsmagazine.com Yearly subscriptions $30.00 for 6 issues. DIMENSIONS IS AN EYE-OPENING MAGAZINE. WHILE IT IS PRIMARILY ORIENTED TOWARDS MALE FA'S (FAT ADMIRERS), THERE ARE A LOT OF SIZE-POSITIVE IMAGES FOR THE GENERAL PUBLIC. IT ALSO HAS INSPIRED MANY FAT WOMEN TOWARDS HAVING A HIGHER SELF-ESTEEM ABOUT THEIR BODIES. LOTS OF FASHIONS, ESPECIALLY LINGERIE AND REVEALING STYLES. DIMENSIONS IS ALSO AN ON-LINE MAGAZINE.

Radiance The Magazine for Large Women. Editor/Publisher: Alice Ansfield. P.O. Box 30246, Oakland, CA 94604. 510-482-0680. Website: www.radiancemagazine.com Yearly subscriptions $20.00 for 4 issues. RADIANCE MAGAZINE IS A CENTERPIECE IN THE SIZE-ACCEPTANCE MOVEMENT. IT IS A VERY SIZE-POSITIVE, SIZE-ACCEPTING, AND WOMEN SUPPORTIVE MAGAZINE. FASHIONS AND SIZE-POSITIVE ART ARE FEATURED, AS WELL AS MANY OTHER TOPICS. RADIANCE ENCOURAGES NON-PROFESSIONAL PLUS AND SUPERSIZE WOMEN TO MODEL FOR THEM. AS OF THIS WRITING, RADIANCE IS CHANGING OVER TO AN ON-LINE MAGAZINE.

REFERENCE DIRECTORIES

THERE ARE A NUMBER OF REFERENCE DIRECTORIES FOR CLOTHING AND ACCESSORIES FOR BOTH PLUS AND SUPERSIZE WOMEN. PAST ONES INCLUDE Full-Figure Fashion Directory-Cathy S Cooper. (1988), Royal Resources by Janice Herrick (1993, 1994), AND MOST RECENTLY, Sandie's Clothesline-Sandie Sabo. DIMENSIONS MAGAZINE'S FASHION EDITOR IS CURRENTLY STILL OFFERING HER CYBER-BOUTIQUE Sandie s Boutique http://www.zaftig-2000.com/sandie. Email: Zaftig2k@aol.com.

SEVERAL RECENT PUBLICATIONS INCLUDE:

The Directory of Resources for Large-Sized Women. $4.95 from Carrie & Joan. P.O. Box 60417, Florence, MA. 01062. www.findinfo.com/large.htm

The Full-Figured Woman s Resource Guide. 272 pages $21.95. Voluptuous Woman Company. 240-568-3890 www.volupwoman.com.

Kelly Bliss Plus Size Yellow Pages HAS BRIDAL, COSTUME, FOOTWEAR, FORMALWEAR, JEWELRY AND ACCESSORIES, JUNIORS, LINGERIE, MATERNITY, SEW YOUR OWN, SWIMWEAR, TEE SHIRTS, USED AND CONSIGNMENT, WOMEN'S CLOTHING. http://www.kellybliss.com.

THE MOST EXTENSIVE ONE TODAY IS, IN MY OPINION: **Judy Sullivan's book, Size Wise: A Catalogue of More Than 1000 Resources for Living With Confidence and Comfort at Any Size. $12.00 . website: www.sizewise.com.**

THIS IS, IN MY OPINION, THE BEST RESOURCE BECAUSE SHE KEEPS CURRENT WITH ALL THE MANY SMALL MANUFACTURERS, NOTING WHEN THEY GO OUT OF BUSINESS, AND INTRODUCING NEWCOMERS. SHE FREQUENTLY AND REGULARLY UPDATES HER WEBSITE, WHICH INCLUDES AN EXTENSIVE LISTING OF MAIL-ORDER CLOTHING CATALOGUES AND SUPPLIERS. LONG-TIME FAVORITES ARE:

Dion-Jones 312-243-4333 (email: dion-jons@netpad.com)
Full Bloom 303-873-9277.
Making It Big toll-free 877-644-1995 (www.bigwomen.com).
Sweeter Measures 819 Front Street Box 340 Gibbon, NE 68840 (308-468-5156).
Peggy Lutz Designs, now Peggy Lutz Plus 1-800-498-3294. 707-824-1634; www.plus-size.com.

SOME OF THE MOST CURRENT AND MOST POPULAR ONES INCLUDE:

Astarte Woman 310-373-0638.
Barb's Large and Lovely, 636-939-4070 www.BLL.com.
Big on Batik Sarongwear 1-888-411-9790 www.bigonbatik.com.
Belle Lingerie Plus 201-447-1619.
Decent Exposures 1-800-524-4949 www.decentexposures.com.
Junonia 1-800-671-0175, www.junonia.com.
Laughing Sisters 1-858-272-1976. laughingsisters@yahoo.com.
Love Your Peaches Clothing Co. Toll Free 1-888-274-7499 www.loveyourpeaches.com.
Myles Ahead 1-888-695-3724 www.Mylesahead.com.
Pickles and Ice Cream Toll-free 1-888-44-PICKLES. www.plusmaternity.com.
Plus Active Wear Toll-free 1-877-994-5353.
Plus Woman 1-800-628-5525 www.pluswoman.com.
Silhouettes 1-800-704-3322 www.silhouettes.com.
Simply Southwest 1-800-447-6177.
Sweet Magnolia Lingerie 1-800-336-2300.
Ulla Popken 1-800-245-8552.

SPECIAL SITES:

Amplestuff: Make Your World Fit You. P.O. Box 116, Bearsville, NY 12409. FOUNDED BY BILL FABREY AND NANCY SUMMER IN 1988, IT OFFERS HOSPITAL GOWNS, BRA LINERS, SOCKS, APRONS, CLOTHES HANGERS, FANNY PACKS, AND MORE. **Website: http://www.amplestuff.com. Email: Amplestuff@aol.com. 845-679-3316.**

Venus Imaging Education: image and lifestyle seminars for women IS AN ONLINE COMMUNITY, BOUTIQUE AND PRESENTS EVENTS FOR WOMEN AND TEENS SIZES 12 AND UP . TOPICS INCLUDE SELF ESTEEM, FASHION, BEAUTY, CAREER, HEALTHY LIFESTYLES, PLUS-SIZE MODELING, THE DIVA BOUTIQUE. **360-882-4416. Website: http://www.VenusDivas.com**

ORGANIZATIONS

NAAFA: National Association to Advance Fat Acceptance P.O. Box 188620 Sacramento, CA 95818. Phone: 1.916.558.6880. hppt://www .Naafa.org NAAFA IS A NONPROFIT HUMAN RIGHTS ORGANIZATION DEDICATED TO IMPROVING THE LIFE OF FAT PEOPLE. IT WAS STARTED IN 1969 BY WILLIAM J. FABREY. NAAFA HAS BEEN A PRIME MOVER IN ESTABLISHING A SIZE ACCEPTANCE COMMUNITY WORLDWIDE. NAAFA CONVENTIONS OFFER FASHION SHOWS ALONG WITH PLUS AND SUPERSIZE CLOTHING VENDORS. MANY WOMEN SAVE UP ALL YEAR TO BUY A NEW WARDROBE AT A NAAFA TRUNK SHOW!

INDEX

INDEX OF ARTISTS

INDEX OF MODELS

ABOUT THE AUTHOR

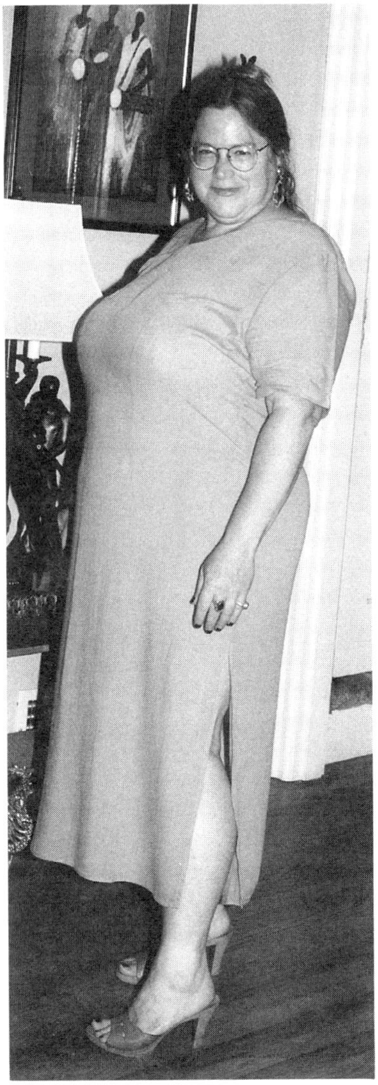

Linda S. Kanzinger is the owner of The Alcott Press, a self-publishing house specializing in clothing and textiles. She is also the author of four books: *The Complete Book of Fabric Painting* 1986, (OP), *The Complete Book of Fabric Painting, rev and expanded,* 1993, *Fabric Painting Resources: 1001 Products and Resources for the Fabric Painter and Surface Designer,* 1994, and the current *Size-Positive Style! Clothing for the Plus* and Supersize Woman.* She has been a writer since her early teens, and a publisher for sixteen years. Her interest in clothing for the fat woman is a long-standing one, and continues into future writing. Other interests include explorations and adventures in the sun in the Eastern Cascades, nature photography, and homesteading. She says "to order directly, just write a check to The Alcott Press for $28.50 PP, and I'll send you a book!"